DAVID TIPLING
THE BIRD PHOTOGRAPHY FIELD GUIDE

The **essential handbook** for capturing birds with your digital SLR

ELSEVIER

AMSTERDAM • BOSTON • HEIDELBERG • LONDON
NEW YORK • OXFORD • PARIS • SAN DIEGO
SAN FRANCISCO • SINGAPORE • SYDNEY • TOKYO

Focal Press is an imprint of Elsevier

Focal
Press

Focal Press is an imprint of Elsevier

30 Corporate Drive, Suite 400, Burlington,
MA 01803, USA

This book was conceived, designed, and produced by
Ilex Press Limited
210 High Street, Lewes, BN7 2NS, UK

Publisher: Alastair Campbell
Creative Director: Peter Bridgewater
Associate Publisher: Adam Juniper
Managing Editor: Natalia Price-Cabrera
Editorial Assistant: Tara Gallagher
Editor: Steve Luck
Senior Designer: James Hollywell
Designer: JC Lanaway
Color Origination: Ivy Press Reprographics

Library of Congress Cataloging-in-Publication Data:
A catalog record for this book is available from
the Library of Congress.

ISBN: 978-0-240-81776-7

For information on all Focal Press publications
visit our website at: *www.focalpress.com*

Printed and bound in China

10 11 12 13 14 5 4 3 2 1

CONTENTS

Foreword	6
Introduction	8
Equipment	**12**
What Digital Camera do I Need?	14
Digital SLRs	18
Digiscoping Equipment	20
Telephoto Lenses	24
Zoom Lenses	28
Teleconverters	30
Wide-angle Lenses	32
Tripods	34
Tripod Heads	36
Beanbags and Window Mounts	38
Understanding Exposure	40
Exposure and Histograms	44
Freezing Action	48
Motion Blur	50
Understanding Depth of Field	52
Memory Cards	54
File Formats	56
Which Format—Raw or JPEG?	58
Taking Care of Equipment	60

Photographing Birds   **62**
Backyard Birds   64
Urban Environments   70
Seabirds   72
Wildfowl and other Waterbirds   74
Birds of Prey   76
Game Birds, Crakes, and Rails   80
Shorebirds   82
Passerines   84
Captive Birds in
  Natural Surroundings   86
Birds in Flight   88
Shooting Low   90
Lighting   92
Capturing Action   98
Stalking and Field Craft   100
Blinds   104
Remote-control Photography   110
Traveling with your Gear by Air   112
Choosing Bird
  Photography Vacations   114
Digiscoping Techniques
  in the Field   116
In the Field—A Personal
  Experience   118

Digital Photo Editing   **120**
Computer Hardware   122
Editing Software and Working
  with Color   126
Importing, Sorting and Editing   130
Processing a Raw Image   134
Improving Composition   142
Adjusting Exposure, Contrast,
  and Color   146
Using Curves   152
The Clone Stamp and
  Healing Brush   154
Resizing and Output Formats   156
Sharpening   158
Printing   162
Getting Published   166
Long-term Picture Storage   172
Bird Photography and Ethics   174

Reference   **178**
Glossary   180
Index   186
Picture Credits   192

Foreword

Never in the history of ornithology has a technological revolution occurred with such lightning speed and profound impact as the arrival of the digital camera. Until recently it was professional photographers who produced most of the informative images found in books, journals, magazines, and on the Internet. The financial outlay, advanced technical skills, and patience required to capture outstanding bird pictures were prohibitive to most amateur photographers. Today, digital equipment and software allow even casual naturalists to produce both beautiful and useful pictures of birds, with only modest investments in resources, time, and practice. Moreover, the Internet now provides a readily available global forum for these images. This "democratization" of photography now produces a tremendous wealth of new information on identification, plumage variation, behavior, distribution, and ecology of birds.

While the move to digital allows the amateur access to the previously exclusive world of the professional photographer, regularly achieving award-winning shots requires a lifetime's dedication. David Tipling comes from this position to share his hard-won expertise, so that this resulting book is an amazing treasure trove of hardware advice, field tricks, artistic nuances, and even editing techniques—all fantastically useful to the amateur and professional alike.

Tipling's numerous awards are richly deserved, for his pictures are both technically superb and brilliantly composed. Often with elegant photographic structure, he captures birds absorbed in their daily rituals. Thus, each picture teaches us something about the bird while also evoking our deeper appreciation for the beauty of life. Thanks to the scores of practical hints presented in this book, the rest of us can now share in his skill.

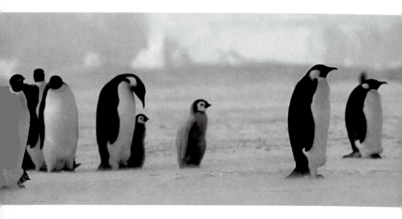

Professionals and amateurs alike will want to consult this book, and I predict that the results will be visible all over the Internet before long. I, for one, cannot wait to get back outside and use some of Tipling's advice to improve my own, humble photographic efforts in the scrubs of Florida and the swamps of Arkansas.

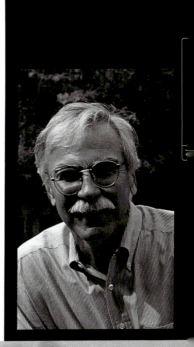

Dr. John W. Fitzpatrick
Director, Cornell Lab of Ornithology

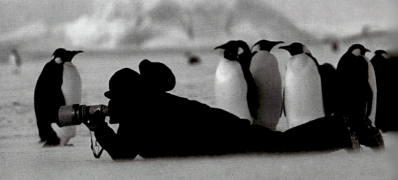

Introduction

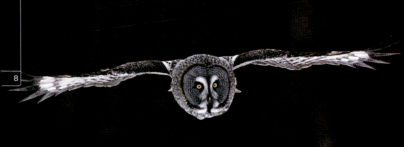

Twenty-five years ago I picked up a camera for the first time, and armed with this and a telephoto lens, I set out to photograph birds. I had little idea of how to take good pictures, other than realizing I needed to get close. My hunting grounds were the fields and lakes near my home in the southeast of England's countryside. Here I honed my skills, studied the local birds, began to understand their behavior, and so slowly learned how to approach birds without causing alarm.

Like many who have caught the bird photography bug, I became hooked, and I can admit that my pastime took over my life. My shameless addiction lasts to this day, and my desire to take pictures burns as bright now as it has ever done.

Many technological advances have come along over the last quarter of a century. When I started, most bird photographers shot in black and white, autofocus (AF) lenses had not been invented, and the digital age was science fiction. However, while the tools of the trade may have changed, many of the techniques used in our wonderful pursuit have not.

What has changed is the ability to photograph birds successfully with the aid of modern digital equipment. Never before have we had so much control over the finished image—whether you are a photographer wanting to create artistic images or a birdwatcher with a desire to record what you see, the opportunities made available by ever-improving cameras and lenses continually push the boundaries of what is possible. The digital revolution has not only raised standards in bird photography but has also encouraged a whole new audience of birdwatchers to pick up a camera and try their hand at this thrilling pursuit.

The jargon-filled world of digital photography can seem daunting at first—bits and bytes, Levels and Curves, histograms and file formats, all help create a barrier that can seem a difficult hurdle to jump. But fear not; my aim in this book is to break down those barriers in easy steps.

This book will take you through the process of choosing the right gear so you can find exactly what you need, it will detail the actual business of photographing birds, and it

BELOW Photographing waders in flight is demanding, so being able to check composition and sharpness as you shoot is a great improvement on the old film approach. This avocet was one of a number of successful flight shots taken in spring from one of the public blinds at Minsmere in Suffolk, U.K.

500mm lens; ISO 100; 1/1000 sec at ƒ/5.6

LEFT After a long wait this great gray owl floated out of a dark Finnish forest straight toward my camera.

500mm lens; handheld; ISO 200; 1/500 sec at ƒ/4

will then teach how to deal with your pictures once you are home. To make life simple, the imaging software used for Section 3 is the latest version of Adobe Photoshop® (CS5 at the time of this writing). Although there are a number of options to choose from when processing digital images, Photoshop is the clear market leader and the most advanced application available. If you use Photoshop Elements, nearly all the processes described for the full version can be made in Elements using the same tools.

Why digital photography?

If you shoot digitally already, you probably don't need this question answered. However, if you are taking up photography and deciding between digital and film, or thinking of swapping from film to digital, then here are a few reasons to convince you that the digital format is the future of bird photography, simply because it provides so many more opportunities than a film-based approach.

Perhaps the greatest argument for using digital photography is the instant access to your image, allowing you to fine-tune as you photograph. Getting exposures right was a big bugbear with film photographers. Now, by using the controls on your camera, an exposure can be perfected as you shoot by viewing the images on the back of your camera to decide whether you like the composition or not. This ability to immediately view what you have taken gives instant gratification. No more long waits for films to come back from the lab.

Once you connect your camera to the computer, you can edit, delete, enhance, and make prints from your images—all within minutes of having taken the photograph.

Many digital SLRs have cropped sensors (see page 16) that, in effect, act as extra magnification, bringing wary birds closer to the camera. Added flexibility comes in the form of being able to change film speeds

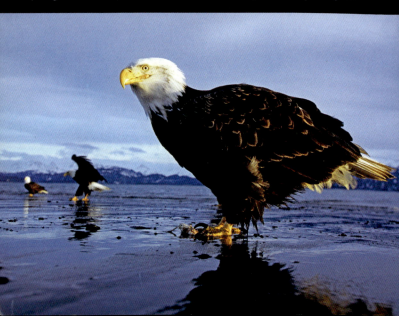

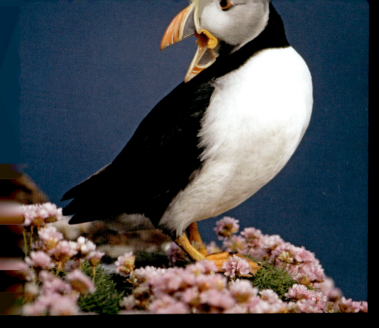

LEFT You can create arresting images of birds with the simplest of equipment—your imagination is the most important ingredient. This bald eagle on the beach at Homer in Alaska's Kachemak Bay was photographed laying on the wet sand to gain this intimate view.

7–35mm zoom lens; ISO 100; 1/125 sec at f/8

ABOVE Puffin among thrift, photographed in Scotland.

600mm lens; ISO 100; 1/500 sec at f/5.6

between shots, and because a digital sensor is far more sensitive to light than film, it is much easier to capture dramatic action using faster shutter speeds and plenty of depth of field.

Running costs are another big factor in digital photography's increasing success. While a good system may not be cheap to set up, once you have all the equipment necessary, you can take as many pictures as you like without worrying about film and processing costs. Pictures in the digital format are easy to share with friends and post on the World Wide Web, and they can be printed with

EQUIPMENT

While you will hear many declare it is not the equipment you use but the person behind the came that produces great bird photographs, it is also true that you do need the right tools for this job. Howeve artistic you might be, and however good your field craft, without the right camera and lens you will find yourself at an immediate disadvantage.

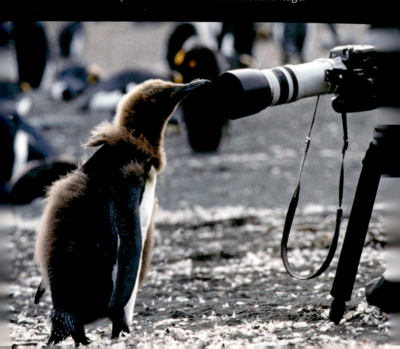

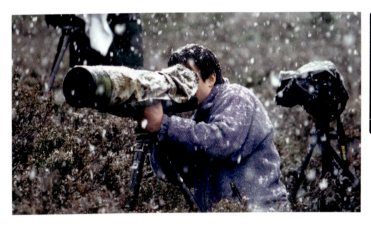

You do not need a vast arsenal of lenses to cover all eventualities. My camera bag contains three lenses that I use 95 percent of the time: a short focal-length zoom of 17–35mm, a medium telephoto zoom of 70–200mm, and a long telephoto 500mm lens. The lens dictates the style of the picture and how close you need to get to your subject, while the camera body you choose is simply the box that captures and stores your image.

Choosing equipment if you are new to photography can seem a confusing task. Like computers, digital SLRs are continually evolving and can become outdated quite quickly. The important consideration is to buy into a system that offers both flexibility for lens choice and the latest technology. The well-trodden path is to choose products from one of the major manufacturers, and I would recommend Canon, Nikon or Sony, since no other brand comes close to these for offering the same range of lenses desirable for bird photography and digital camera technology that is upgraded regularly.

OPPOSITE A king penguin investigates my lens.

ABOVE In adverse weather you should take care to protect your equipment.

The good news when buying equipment is that there are many retailers out there competing for your business. Shop around, particularly on the Internet, and don't accept the published prices retailers advertise; if buying a complete outfit, good deals can be struck by haggling and playing retailers against each other. Don't dismiss buying secondhand gear: there is a big market for used cameras and lenses, and most photographers do look after their equipment. Buying a secondhand digital camera from a private seller without the ability to fully test it might be risky, but lenses can easily be inspected before purchasing. Most dealers will provide insurance on secondhand equipment in the case of a fault being discovered.

What Digital Camera Do I Need?

There is an ever-increasing and almost bewildering range of digital cameras available. Take time to find out which is best for you, in terms of both your photography needs and your budget, and be prepared to shop around.

It used to be that digital cameras could be conveniently divided into two broad categories: the compact—historically used by the general population for taking pictures on vacation—and the digital single lens reflex (DSLR). The latter being used by more serious photographers, including professionals, and the camera of choice for bird photography.

The reasons for this were clear cut. A DSLR allows you to change lenses and most importantly is backed up by a good choice of long telephoto lenses, a necessity for bird photography. When you look through the viewfinder of a DSLR, what you see in the frame is the actual view through the lens; further, you have the ability to check depth of field (how much of the scene is in focus), and you can easily adjust settings for creating

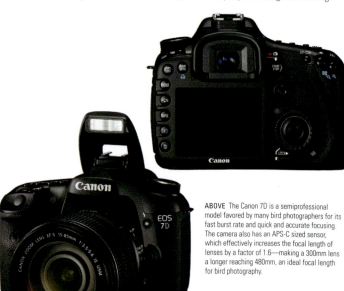

ABOVE The Canon 7D is a semiprofessional model favored by many bird photographers for its fast burst rate and quick and accurate focusing. The camera also has an APS-C sized sensor, which effectively increases the focal length of lenses by a factor of 1.6—making a 300mm lens a longer reaching 480mm, an ideal focal length for bird photography.

effects, whether you want to freeze action, blur motion, or control the depth of field.

Digital compact cameras were once considered far more limited; you couldn't change their lenses, and although many have zoom lenses, most were not "long" enough for photographing birds. Furthermore, and most importantly they did not deliver the image quality of DSLRs. Even though many can match a DSLR in terms of the number of pixels on the sensors, the sensors and pixels themselves are much smaller, resulting in poorer image quality. Although many of these drawbacks still hold true for the vast majority of "point-and-shoot" compact cameras, a new breed of "compact" camera is making itself known in the market.

In 2008 Panasonic released the Lumix DMC-G1, the first Micro Four Thirds camera. It has no mirror and prism, and therefore no optical viewfinder. The user frames the shot using either an electronic viewfinder (EVF) or

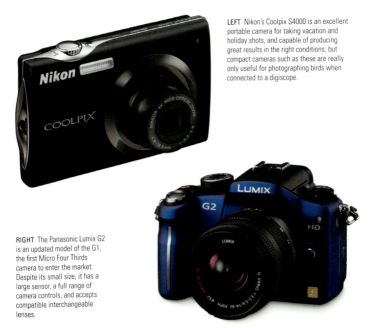

LEFT Nikon's Coolpix S4000 is an excellent portable camera for taking vacation and holiday shots, and capable of producing great results in the right conditions; but compact cameras such as these are really only useful for photographing birds when connected to a digiscope.

RIGHT The Panasonic Lumix G2 is an updated model of the G1, the first Micro Four Thirds camera to enter the market. Despite its small size, it has a large sensor, a full range of camera controls, and accepts compatible interchangeable lenses.

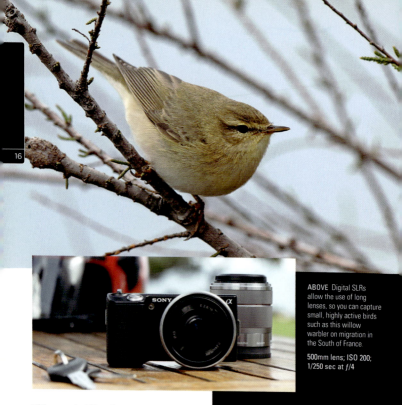

ABOVE Digital SLRs allow the use of long lenses, so you can capture small, highly active birds such as this willow warbler on migration in the South of France.

500mm lens; ISO 200; 1/250 sec at f/4

LCD screen, just like all compact cameras. But unlike other compacts Panasonic's Micro Four Thirds cameras, and those now made by Olympus, can use interchangeable lenses, have sensors nine times larger than an average compact, and offer the same level of control as many entry-level DSLRs—all in a much smaller package.

For a while Panasonic and Olympus were the only two manufacturers exploiting the Micro Four Thirds format. However, more recently Samsung and Sony—historically

ABOVE In their bid to attract a new breed of photographer, Sony have eschewed the traditional look of DSLRs with their new range of compact interchangeable lens cameras. Despite their small size, the NEX cameras feature an APS-C-sized sensor, the same size as those found in all entry-level and semi-professional DSLRs.

RIGHT The flexibility of DSLRs means more possibilities for creativity. I used a slow shutter speed to create motion blur when photographing this greater roadrunner in New Mexico.

500mm lens; ISO 100; 1/30 sec at f/16

electronics companies rather than camera manufacturers—have entered the mirrorless interchangeable lens camera market with new camera models. Despite their small sizes—Sony's NEX models in particular are extremely compact—these new models feature the larger APS-C-sized sensors found in DSLRs, with the potential to match such cameras in terms of image quality.

In terms of using such cameras for bird photography, at present dedicated lenses are limited to medium telephoto, which doesn't always get you close enough to the subject, and they are not as responsive in the field as DSLRs. In the future, longer focal length lenses may well become available, and as processing speeds improve making them faster, such cameras could become a viable, lightweight alternative to entry-level DSLRs. There's no doubting that the holy grail of compactness coupled with high image quality, although perhaps not fully realized, is certainly within reach.

One region in which compact digital cameras—both point and shoot and interchangeable lens compacts—do come into their own in bird photography is in digiscoping (see page 20), where a compact camera is married with a telescope to take high-magnification images, very often with great success.

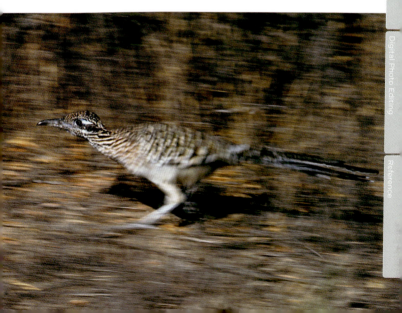

Digital SLRs

Even when you've decided on a DSLR over another type of camera, there are a number of options to be explored before making your final choice. For successful bird photography, some of the available features need to meet high standards.

Sensors in DSLRs come in two formats: they are either the same size as a 35mm frame and are known as "full frame," or they come in a smaller size (the most common) and are known as "cropped sensors." Full-frame sensors will provide marginally better image quality, although this may only be apparent in large, professional prints.

A benefit of smaller sensors is the well-known cropping effect—they give the result of using a longer lens than in reality: for example, a 500mm lens when used with a camera that gives an effective 750mm zoom has a cropped frame to the factor of 1.5x. This is obviously a huge advantage to the bird photographer, particularly when working with small birds or those that are hard to approach.

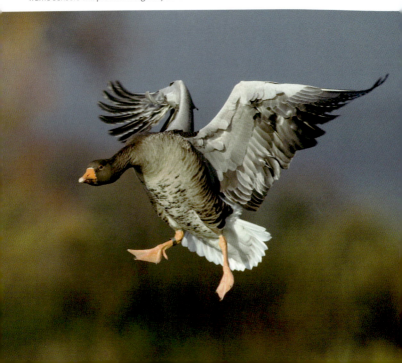

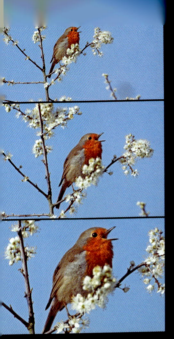

Choosing a DSLR

When choosing a DSLR, there are a number of factors to take into account:

1 Does pixel count matter?

Pixels are the building blocks of an image—the more pixels a sensor has, the higher the resolution, and the more detail that will be recorded; this in turn dictates the size of the prints you can get. However, with even entry-level DSLRs now boasting sensors with 15 megapixels, large poster-sized prints are now easily achievable. However, the benefit of higher resolution—some DSLRs now feature 24 megapixels—is that you can crop a picture more without losing a lot of quality. The drawback to cameras with such large sensors, however, is the size of the files they produce. Large files use up more space on the memory card, as well as on your computer, and also take longer to process during post-production.

2 How many frames per second?

Birds are often in motion; feeding, fighting, bathing, flying. To capture action, it is a big advantage to be able to shoot pictures in quick succession, and achieving at least four or five frames per second is desirable. If there are fewer than that, you will miss potential shots.

3 What is the burst depth?

This is the number of frames your camera will shoot before the buffer fills up and the camera prevents you from taking any more pictures until the buffer starts to empty. Digital cameras process a lot of information, and the more pixels you have, the longer your camera may take to process this information. The burst depth varies between makes of camera, and as technology improves it is becoming less of an issue.

While the above points are important, so too is how the camera feels in your hand. When you use it with a long telephoto lens on a tripod, does it feel balanced? Are the controls readily accessible? Is it right for the size of your hands? Does it feature weather sealing? These are factors not to be ignored.

LEFT Capturing action successfully, such as this greylag goose's landing at Caerlaverock in Scotland, requires a digital SLR with a good burst rate and burst depth. This means you can capture as many images as possible as you follow the bird with your lens.

500mm lens; ISO 100; 1/1000 sec at f/4

ABOVE These pictures illustrate how the cropping effect works in order to give you a larger bird in the frame. The first image shows the effect of the robin photographed with a full-frame sensor; the second and third emulate the effect with cropped sensors—1.3 x and 1.6 x respectively. The robin shown here was photographed in spring in Kent, England.

500mm lens; ISO 100; 1/500 sec at f/6.3

Digiscoping Equipment

Compact digital cameras, in particular the more recent compact interchangeable lens cameras, really come into their own in digiscoping, which enables extraordinary close-ups of birds to be captured. If you do decide to buy a compact for this reason, make sure that the zoom offered is optical, not digital.

Digiscoping has brought bird photography to the masses. Simply, it is the marriage of either a compact camera or DSLR to a telescope, of the type commonly used by birdwatchers, to take pictures. Bird magazines are now packed with images taken by this method. For many it is an affordable stepping stone to serious bird photography, while

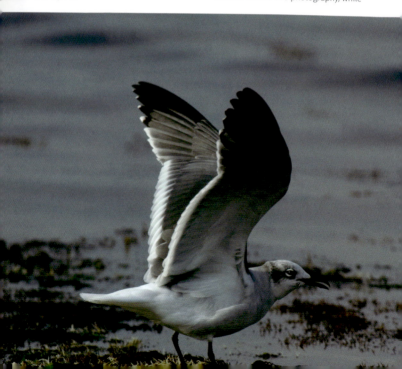

others find it allows them to grab pictures of particular birds when out in the field.

Digiscoping started when birdwatchers began to experiment with placing their compact cameras against the eyepiece of their telescope when focused on a perched bird. Remarkable results were achieved, and the craze has now led to custom adapter mounts being manufactured to fix compact cameras and DSLRs to the scope. Of course, holding a compact to the scope's eyepiece still works, but by using a special adapter, more control can be gained over the focusing and composing of the image.

To go digiscoping you need a compact camera, as already discussed earlier. You also need a good-quality telescope with an eyepiece of 20–30x. The scope should ideally have a large objective lens of at least 77mm—high definition glass will help enormously—and this all needs to be mounted on a sturdy tripod. Finally, get yourself a remote release lead, which will help to avoid camera shake when using extremely high magnifications or slower shutter speeds.

You can just hold any old compact up to the eyepiece of your scope and get very acceptable results; however, for more control over your picture-taking, using an adapter is recommended. Adapters fit between the camera and telescope eyepiece, usually by being screwed into the camera's lens filter thread. The image may not always be very bright, but using a low-magnification eyepiece—ideally nothing larger than 30x—on your scope helps. These also assist in both finding the bird and avoiding too much lens shake, and most low-magnification eyepieces give ample power. One point to remember when choosing a compact camera is to ensure that the front lens element is smaller than your telescope's eyepiece, otherwise vignetting will be a big problem.

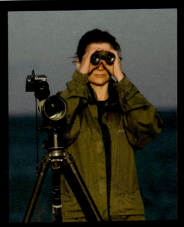

LEFT Digiscoping is very popular with birdwatchers wanting to capture images of vagrant birds, such as this laughing gull sporting its winter plumage. This particular gull is an American species photographed in Greece.

Nikon Coolpix 9500 on Nikon Fieldscope ED 82 with 22x eyepiece; ISO 400; 1/250 sec at f/8

ABOVE Because of the high magnifications involved in digiscoping, you will find it takes time to get used to locating the bird in the camera's viewfinder quickly. I make it a habit to keep the lens at its shortest focal length when searching, only zooming in when I have the bird in sight.

When choosing a compact camera, don't get fooled by the difference between optical zoom and digital zoom—the latter just zooms in on the image, enlarging the picture by sacrificing quality. Go for a camera with an optical zoom; this is a true zoom in that pixels are not sacrificed, and it helps eliminate or reduce vignetting. Even on low zoom settings, the magnification is far beyond anything possible with conventional telephoto lenses—for example, a 4x zoom combined with a 30x eyepiece will give a magnification of 90x.

There are adaptors for using DSLRs on telescopes, but limitations in image quality start to become apparent when using these, as the DSLR's superior picture quality shows up lens imperfections more easily. That said, such a setup is easier to use than a compact, since there is no shutter lag (delay in shutter firing) as found on some compacts, and it is easier to frame the image and focus when looking through a DSLR viewfinder.

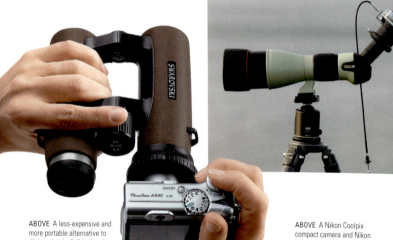

ABOVE A less-expensive and more portable alternative to digiscoping is digibinning, in which a compact camera is temporarily attached to a pair of binoculars. Understandably results are a little more hit and miss than with a tripod-mounted scope, but digibinning is a viable option if you have to travel light.

ABOVE A Nikon Coolpix compact camera and Nikon Fieldscope ED 82 are a typical digiscoping outfit. The Nikon Coolpix is fitted to a bracket that slips onto the eyepiece of the scope. This bracket allows for the zoom lens that extends from the camera when zoomed.

Digiscope camera settings

These are by no means intended to be the
only settings to use, as to some degree
the settings you choose will also depend
on the specific shot. The settings
described here, however will be a good
starting point and provide good results in
most conditions.

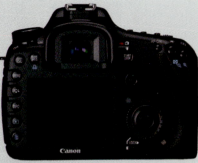

Exposure mode
Avoid using Auto or any of the Program
modes. While these settings may be
appropriate for more general photography,
they're unlikely to give you the best result.
Instead set the camera to the Aperture Priority mode
(A or Av). Manually select the largest aperture setting
(smallest number), and the camera will automatically
select an appropriate shutter speed for the available
light. If light levels are poor and the shutter speed is
too slow (1/60 sec and below) you run the risk of
getting blurred shots. To avoid the blurred effect
increase the ISO setting.

Metering
With bird photography in particular it's absolutely
essential to ensure your subject is accurately exposed.
The best metering options are either spot metering
(which takes an exposure reading entirely from the
central spot) or center-weighted (which sets exposure
primarily on the center spot but will also allow partially
for the background).

White balance
Modern compacts cope very well with a variety of
lighting conditions so leaving the camera on Auto
White Balance will usually provide accurate results.

Autofocus (AF) mode
Most cameras offer a choice between Single AF and
Continuous AF. Although birds are usually moving, use
Single AF as the camera will focus much more quickly
and efficiently.

Image quality
Ideally you want to shoot with the highest-quality
setting, which is Raw. However, if you notice that you
are missing shots due to the amount of time it takes
for the camera to write the data to the memory card,
use JPEG Fine.

Drive mode
Experiment with the camera's Continuous drive mode.
Birds are unpredictable, and with this mode you can
get a burst of shots and select the best pose. However,
you may find that the write speed time is unacceptably
long, in which case revert to Single Shot mode.

Focus mode
The speediest option is Macro, however if the bird is
not the closest object to the lens then you'll need to
switch to Infinity.

Telephoto Lenses

Telephoto lenses come in a variety of sizes, ranging in price from budget to very expensive. A good lens is essential for bird photography, and an added factor is the aperture that comes with the lens; smaller is better.

Many of the birds you set out to photograph will be small, and even the few exceptions such as herons and other large waders appear to be surprisingly small when it comes to getting a decent photograph. When I'm out with my big 500mm lens, I regularly get comments from passersby to the effect that I must be getting a great shot of the bird's eyeball! In truth, however, to get a tight shot of even a relatively large bird like a duck, you need to be not much farther than twenty feet away with a 500mm lens.

Having a long telephoto lens for bird photography is essential, and I suggest you need at least 400mm. There are quite a few photographers who favor 300mm lenses and use teleconverters (see page 30), and if you do a lot of general wildlife photography, this may be a sensible option; however, if birds are your main quarry, 500mm lens is the optimum length. There are a number of reasons for this: longer lenses tend to be substantially heavier and more bulky, so they end up being a real chore to carry when out in the field; they also come with a much higher price tag. A decent 500mm lens, although expensive, will give you the reach for all situations, including small birds such as warblers. When used with a cropped DSLR, you are, although this is not technically correct, in effect extending your

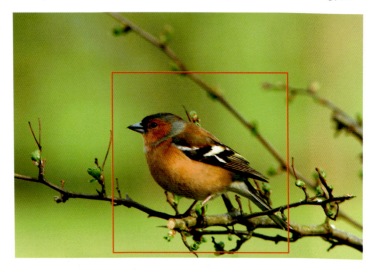

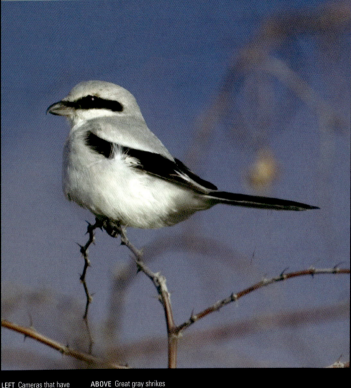

LEFT Cameras that have APS-C-sized sensors, which are smaller than the full-frame (35mm) sensors found in some DSLRs, effectively increase the focal length of the lens, which is ideal when photographing birds from a distance. The red square illustrates the "cropping" effect of such cameras.

ABOVE Great gray shrikes are notoriously difficult to get close to. For this image I had to resort to using a 1.4x converter on my 500mm lens. The image was taken at Lake Kerkini in Greece in winter.

500mm lens; 1.4x converter; ISO 200; 1/320 sec at f/5.6

focal length. Top-of-the-line 500mm lenses come with a maximum aperture of $f/4$; this wide aperture allows plenty of light in, making the lens easy to focus, and the autofocus is snappier when compared to a cheaper lens with a maximum aperture of, say, $f/5.6$.

There are advantages of going for a maximum aperture of $f/4$ over $f/5.6$, although this is only one stop. These are that you not only get better autofocus performance but also the leeway to use reasonably high shutter speeds at the start and end of the day, when the light is at its best. In addition, this aperture gives the ability to use a 1.4x converter for extra reach with small birds, while only losing one stop of light.

There are really plenty of options, even without choosing a 500mm lens. This is particularly true when employing the use of teleconverters. Because many digital camera bodies give a cropping effect, you might find some of these lenses adequate for your photography. A 400mm lens used in conjunction with a camera with a 1.3x crop is going to give you an effective focal length of 520mm, while a 300mm with the same crop becomes a 390mm lens. Good 300mm $f/4$ lenses can be bought for a fraction of the price of the bigger lenses, and a 1.4x teleconverter with a cropped frame camera might be the budget answer.

Pro tip

When purchasing a telephoto lens, pay close attention to the minimum focusing distance of various models. You might think that this is immaterial with a 500 or 600mm lens; however, remember that goldcrests, kinglets, and tiny hummingbirds are actually very small. Even at the minimum focusing distance of my top-notch 500mm lens, such birds are still quite small in the frame.

BELOW The Nikkor AF-S 500mm lens for Nikon cameras is a professional-quality lens with a maximum aperture of $f/4$—making it the ideal lens for bird photography. Unfortunately it comes with a very large price tag.

RIGHT This image of a juvenile wood sandpiper taking off from a pool in Finland was photographed at 4 a.m. My $f/4$ lens gave me a little extra light to help freeze the action.

500mm lens; ISO 200; 1/250 sec at $f/4$

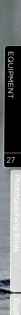

Photographing Birds

Digital Photo Editing

Reference

Zoom Lenses

Zoom lenses are a useful addition to your camera bag, and as with telephoto lenses, you get what you pay for when it comes to speed and the quality of the optics. Zooms are very versatile, particularly in situations where you encounter birds that are tame.

Medium-range telephoto zoom lenses are very useful for bird photography. There are many destinations around the world, such as Florida and the Antarctic, where the birds are so tame that many species can be photographed with a focal length much shorter than 400 or 500mm.

The most popular medium telephoto zoom is the 70- or 80–200mm, which is ideal for all sorts of applications. I carry a 70–200mm lens in my bag as a matter of course and use it regularly, whether for birdscapes or closer shots of tame subjects. The maximum aperture is normally $f/2.8$, which is very useful in low light and for taking advantage of a very shallow depth of field for close-ups with impact.

The shorter zooms, for example 55–120mm and 70–200mm, are ideal for what I call birdscapes—landscapes that include flocks or individual birds. Such images can set a scene beautifully, and some sites lend themselves well to this kind of image; for example the winter flocks of snow and Ross's geese and sandhill cranes in Bosque Del Apache in New Mexico. Here you can stand on observation decks overlooking both roosting ponds and feeding areas, from where some really eye-catching images can be made within the landscape.

Pro tip

If you choose a zoom lens where you pull the barrel up and down, make sure the mechanism is tight enough to prevent accidental zooming when the lens is pointed up and down. These lenses also increase the length of the lens when being zoomed out, which is not always ideal when working with one in a blind.

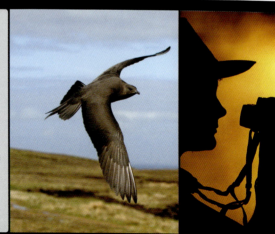

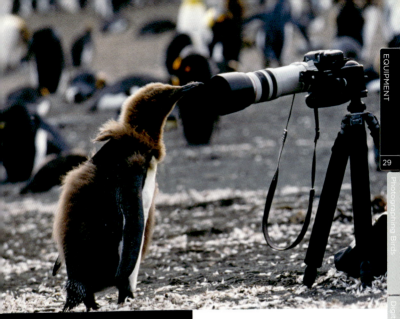

FAR LEFT Medium-length zoom lenses can be useful for flight photography. I used a 70–200mm zoom at 82mm to capture this parasitic jaeger in flight on Scotland's Shetland Isles in spring.

70–200mm zoom; ISO 100; 1/800 sec at ƒ/5.6

LEFT If you want to sell your work, then good images of birdwatchers are always in demand. I use a medium zoom lens for much of this work.

70–200mm zoom lens; ISO 100; 1/250 sec at ƒ/11

ABOVE Zooms are very useful as long as you can get far enough away from the birds! This inquisitive king penguin was inspecting a Canon 100–400mm zoom, photographed on the island of South Georgia.

300mm lens; ISO 100; 1/250 sec at ƒ/5.6

There are plenty of other medium telephoto zooms on the market, such as 75–400mm, 100–400mm, 100–300mm, and so on. The disadvantages of some of these are their variable apertures: for example, a 100–300mm may have a maximum aperture of ƒ/4 at the 100mm range, but this may decrease to ƒ/5.6 at the 300mm range. The advantage of these, however, is in their cost, as they are normally a lot more affordable than the fast ƒ/2.8 lenses.

The price of a new fast lens may be prohibitive, so don't dismiss buying used equipment. Because of their popularity, there are always a few available, and not only are you likely to save yourself a substantial amount of money but there is also a lot less to go wrong in a lens than in a camera body, so the risk of the equipment failing is much smaller.

Teleconverters

Achieve further magnification by using a teleconverter, but be careful, because camera shake and a lack of light reaching the camera's sensor may become apparent in your photographs. Low-quality converters should be avoided.

Teleconverters act as magnifiers that fit between the camera and the lens. Photographers give these all sorts of names, "converters" being the most commonly used. They normally come as either 1.4x or 2x, although Nikon makes a 1.7x version as well. In effect, you are multiplying the focal length of your lens by a factor of two when you use a 2x, so 500mm becomes 1000mm and so on.

The catch with converters is that the loss of light slows the lens down. When a 1.4x converter is used, you lose one stop of light, so your $f/4$ lens becomes a $f/5.6$; and with a 2x you lose two stops, so it becomes an $f/8$. This increase in focal length means you need to remember to use a fast enough shutter speed to avoid camera shake.

I often use my 1.4x converter but rarely my 2x, and there is a good reason for this. The doubling of magnification that a 2x brings means a much faster shutter speed is required to avoid camera shake, but because you have already lost two stops of light, you may find that unless the conditions are bright you will start to struggle with speed, having a decent tripod then becomes indispensable. Of course you can increase the ISO to allow for faster shutter speeds, but it's good practice to use as low an ISO as possible to reduce the amount of noise in your image (see page 138).

Autofocus will be slowed down with converters, quite drastically with a 2x but less so with the 1.4x. This is because of the reduction in light, which affects performance. Some zoom lenses can struggle with picture

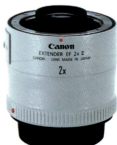

LEFT Teleconverters are small lenses that further magnify the image found by your telephoto or zoom lens. This is the Canon Extender EF 2X II.

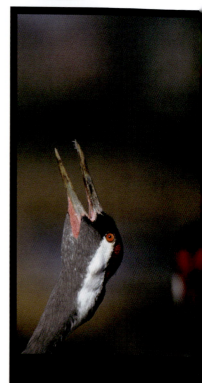

quality when coupled with converters, though this is not noticeable when using the top-of-the-range lenses. I have used a 1.4x on my 70–200mm zoom to great effect, as this makes for a really useful combination for handheld flight shots.

You should always use the dedicated converters produced by your lens manufacturer; those produced by Canon or Nikon have the best glass and optical coatings to give an optimum result. Independent lens manufacturers make converters, but these are generally disappointing in comparison, and when using them you are likely to see a big drop-off in the image quality of your photographs. The same is true if you use a top-class converter on a cheap lens: the results will just not be as you had hoped.

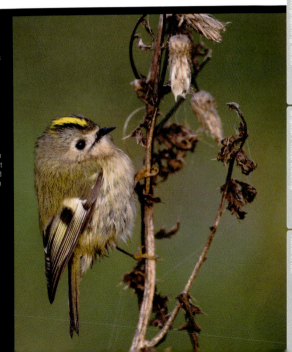

LEFT This common crane, photographed in Sweden, started to call with another bird visible farther back. By using a 1.4x converter I was able to frame the closest bird, so that the one farther away appeared to be a mirrored reflection.

500mm lens with 1.4x converter; ISO 100; 1/500 sec at *f*/4

RIGHT The goldcrest is Europe's smallest bird. Even at the closest focusing point for my 500mm lens, the bird still appeared quite small in the frame. By adding a 1.4x converter, I was able to boost the image size without having to crop too drastically once the image was on my screen.

500mm lens; ISO 320; 1/320 sec at *f*/4

Wide-angle Lenses

A wide-angle lens provides the bird photographer with another option, that of placing the subject in context, as opposed to filling the frame. Extreme wide-angle lenses, such as fish-eyes, can be used very creatively to make strikingly unusual images.

You might think wide-angle lenses are superfluous to bird photography. Well, think again. Wide-angle lenses can be used to great effect in creating really eye-catching bird portraits, particularly with superwide or fish-eye lenses. The obvious use of a wide-angle lens is to photograph a bird within a wider scene—and this can add an interesting narrative. What I like to do, especially with fish-eye lenses, is to lure a bird so close to the lens that it is almost touching; this distorts the angles of the head a little and makes for a shot full of impact.

There are bound to be locations close to where you live where some birds are extremely tame. The obvious examples are parks in towns and cities: those with ponds and lakes, for example, almost always have tame waterfowl in them. The great thing about such places is the birds' readiness to come close when food is waved in front of their beaks. For example, St. James's Park in central London is a great place for bird photography, especially for taking wide-angle shots. The birds are easy to approach and won't fly off as you move about taking photographs of them.

The closer your wide-angle lens focuses the better: ideal length for creating images is 24mm or less—more than this and you lose the effect. I use a 10mm fish-eye lens on a cropped-frame DSLR, which gives a fullframe equivalent focal length of around 16mm.

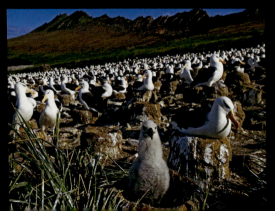

LEFT When shooting this black-browed albatross colony on Steeple Jason Island in the Falkland Islands, I used the young chick as the central focus in the foreground.

17–35mm lens; ISO 100; 1/125 sec at f/16

ABOVE RIGHT Wide angles can be utilized for a variety of shots. Here this road casualty barn owl made a strong foreground, giving the image impact. The car headlights in the background add drama and help to tell the story. Here I rested my camera on a beanbag for stability.

17mm lens; ISO 100; 1/45 sec at f/5.6

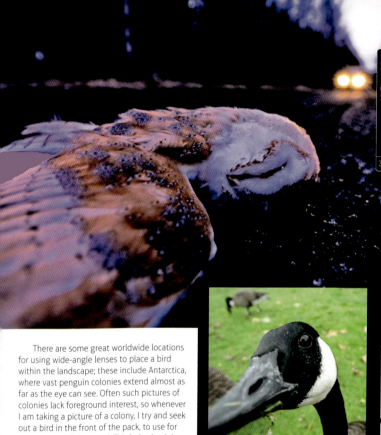

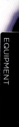

There are some great worldwide locations for using wide-angle lenses to place a bird within the landscape; these include Antarctica, where vast penguin colonies extend almost as far as the eye can see. Often such pictures of colonies lack foreground interest, so whenever I am taking a picture of a colony, I try and seek out a bird in the front of the pack, to use for impact in the foreground. This helps lead the eye into the picture and can also encourage a sense of scale. I have even used wide angles when photographing very tame bald eagles in Homer, Alaska.

It is easy to get caught up in using your long lens exclusively on a subject, but by stepping back and looking at the wider picture, a wide-angle might be just the job to take a creative image of the bird in its habitat.

ABOVE Using wide-angle and fish-eye lenses close up to tame birds can give some wacky effects. This Canada goose was photographed in St. James's Park in London, having been lured close to the camera with bread.

17–35mm lens; ISO 100
1/250 sec at f/4

Tripods

As a bird photographer who works almost exclusively outdoors and in all weather conditions, you are going to need a tripod that can be carried easily and will stand up to a lot of heavy use. It must also stand firm on uneven terrain.

When using long telephoto lenses, it is essential you use a tripod. Really the only time it is possible to get away with hand-holding these is when taking flight shots with a high shutter speed.

The stability of your tripod is key to the quality of your pictures. You can spend thousands on cameras and telephoto lenses, but if you then try to save with a cheap tripod, it will only prove to be a false economy. A good number of models found in your average camera store are often of poor design and do not last long when used by outdoor

photographers—who punish their equipment rather more than someone operating in a studio. When considering a tripod, give it the wobble test: if it seems flimsy, then it definitely will be no good for supporting a heavy 500mm lens.

There are two manufacturers who stand above the rest for making good, sturdy tripods; they are Manfrotto and Gitzo, and they both offer aluminium and carbon-fiber versions. Clearly a carbon-fiber tripod is going to be relatively light when compared to its metal cousin, but if you decide to go for a carbon-fiber model, make sure it is not too light—if it blows around in the wind it will be useless. The only other drawback with carbon-fiber tripods is the cost: they are usually twice the price of metal tripods, so you need to consider the weight advantages versus cost.

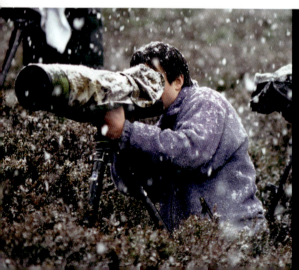

LEFT Using a sturdy tripod with a long lens pays dividends in poor light and adverse weather. Note the lens cover to protect against the snow.

ABOVE RIGHT I used my tripod with legs splayed to capture this low-level portrait of a greater roadrunner sunning itself in New Mexico's Bosque Del Apache Reserve.

500mm lens; ISO 100; 1/250 sec at f/11

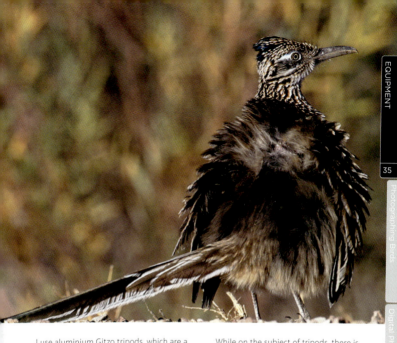

I use aluminium Gitzo tripods, which are a favorite with professionals due to their durability: well-made, well-designed, and easy to operate, they are hard to fault. My recommendation is to go for a model with no central column, since such columns create wobble when extended. It is also a good idea to go for a model where the legs will splay out at right angles, which is really useful when on uneven ground or sitting on a bank, as you can make the tripod very stable by getting just the right angle with your legs. With splayed legs and no central column, you also have a good support for laying on the ground and shooting low-level shots. Those tripods with the central column inverted or jutting out sideways are definitely worth avoiding, since they complicate what is a simple operation.

While on the subject of tripods, there is one other device worthy of investigation for occasional use, and that is the monopod. Using just one leg takes practice with a long lens, but monopods are useful for stalking birds in thick bush, or for using medium telephoto lenses. They are not a substitute for a good tripod, but they are certainly better than using no support at all. As with tripod legs, they come in both aluminium and carbon fiber; the latter is best for monopods as all the weight is concentrated on the one leg, giving it stability despite its lack of weight.

Tripod Heads

With a basic choice of four types of tripod head, you may have to spend some time in camera stores, trying out different models and styles until you find one that feels comfortable with your tripod, camera, and lens.

Once you have your tripod legs, you obviously need a head on which to mount your camera and lens. Heads come in four basic types: the gimbal-style head, pan-and-tilt, video or fluid head, and the ball head. Unlike choosing a set of tripod legs, where there is a clear definition of what is needed, which tripod head you choose is a matter of personal choice. Test the head with your tripod, camera, and lenses and go with the one that you feel gives the most flexibility and stability for your setup.

In my career I have, at one time or another, used all four kinds of tripod heads. For many years I used a pan-and-tilt head, which tilts backward and forward and swivels around, all controlled by a series of knobs. Pan-and-tilt heads are very easy to use and give good stability to long lenses. When looking at these, avoid those that have a long handle to control the forward-and-back movement—these can be very awkward, as they tend to stick into your shoulder when looking through the viewfinder.

Video or fluid heads are similar in effect to pan-and-tilt heads. They have very smooth actions, since the mechanism sits in a viscous fluid; others operate by using a system of springs. They allow various settings for resistance, and are popular with filmmakers as well as stills photographers. The downside is their expense.

My head of choice is the ball-and-socket, commonly referred to as "ball heads." These have just one knob as a control, giving ease of movement in any plane, with a control for setting resistance. They do take a bit of getting used to, but once mastered, they are very versatile. Arca Swiss is perhaps the best-known make and is a high-quality name. Ball heads come in different sizes, so it is imperative to purchase one big enough to take your heaviest lens comfortably.

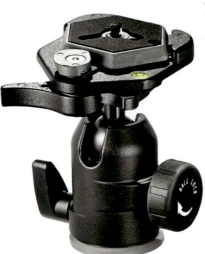

LEFT A ball head combines a simple design with a large amount of flexibility. The circular knob adjusts the mechanism's resistance to cope with different lens weights, and the opposite lever fixes the camera to any position on a horizontal plane.

Finally we come to the gimbal-style heads. The most popular of these is the Wimberley, especially with bird photographers in the United States. It is ideal for long, heavy lenses such as the 500mm and the extra-large, heavy 600mm f/4 models, as the large lump of glass in the end of these has a tendency to tip the lens forward when tension is loosened on other tripod heads.

The Wimberley works by allowing you to align the center of gravity for the lens so that lens and camera are held in perfect balance. This means the lens can pivot in the horizontal and vertical axes with little resistance, so it is great for following birds in flight. The downside is both price and weight. If you do a lot of walking when out shooting bird pictures, the gimbal style may prove too heavy. Remember also that it is a one-trick pony, great for big telephotos, but not suitable for shorter lenses.

The alternative to the Wimberley is its baby brother, the Sidekick, which has the advantage of being small. It is an arm that fits onto a ball head to give you a similar freedom of movement to the Wimberley. The other advantage with this is that you retain the ball head capability, which is more useful for shooting other subjects with shorter lenses.

Whatever system you choose, it is worth investing in quick-release plates. These attach to the lens and slip onto the tripod head, allowing a lens to be fixed or removed very quickly—this might make the difference between grabbing an unexpected shot or not.

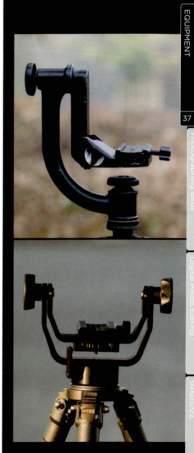

ABOVE Both the Wimberley (top) and the Dietmar Nill (above) tripod heads are excellent for action photography, allowing for smooth panning and a stability not offered by more traditional heads when using long lenses.

Beanbags and Window Mounts

A simple beanbag or window mount is the answer for taking shots while traveling in a vehicle, when a tripod is impractical to use. Both have the advantage of being light and easily transportable.

Cheap and versatile, and an essential piece of your kit if you take pictures when traveling, a beanbag is simply a cloth bag with a zip that you can fill with dried beans or rice. I prefer rice, since it is easily obtainable anywhere in the world. One trick some photographers have is to fill it with bird seed, as you never know when this might come in useful! Make sure that, whatever you use, the bag is filled sufficiently to give good, solid support. Beanbags are ideal for use as supports on window frames in vehicles or as a rest on the lip of a public blind, and I often use them when lying on the ground to take low-level shots.

There are two types of beanbag you can buy, if you decide to purchase rather than make one yourself. They differ in that one is simply a bag, while the other is a double-pocket design. The latter flops conveniently over car window ledges, and the narrow space for the filling at the top helps the bag not to sag. Make sure you buy one with a zip so it can be emptied when traveling, to save on weight. As you're unlikely to be using more than one large lens at a time, there's no need to buy more than one beanbag.

As an alternative to using a beanbag as your support in a car, there are specially designed window clamps on the market. One of the best in terms of design and engineering is the Kirk window mount, made by Kirk Enterprises; the advantage of this over some others is that you can attach your tripod head to the mount. Window mounts have the edge on beanbags when used in a vehicle moving away from the open road, as you can leave your camera and lens set up on the mount, ready for instant action.

Window mounts can also be very useful if you do a lot of photography from public bird blinds. The wooden blinds found on Royal Society for the Protection of Birds (RSPB) reserves in the U.K. often offer good opportunities for photography, and window mounts are frequently ideal for support when shooting from some of these, particularly when seating arrangements sometimes preclude the use of a tripod.

Pro tip

Use beanbags with your long lens to add stability. As well as resting the lens on the bag, rest another on top to prevent any shaking. I have used this technique in wooden blinds and when in a vehicle, when using slow shutter speeds that create motion blur.

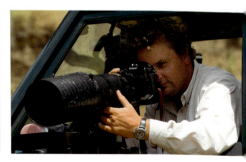

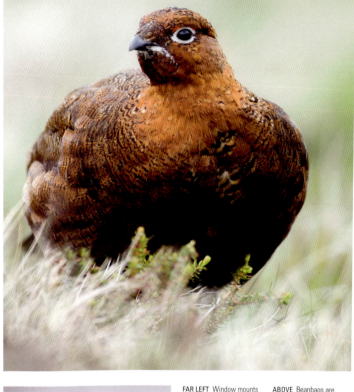

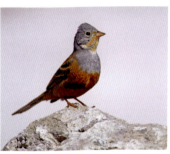

FAR LEFT Window mounts can be very useful if you take a lot of pictures from your vehicle.

LEFT I photographed this Cretzchmar's bunting in Greece resting my telephoto lens on a beanbag placed on a rock.

500mm lens; ISO 100; 1/800 sec at f/5.6

ABOVE Beanbags are flexible and ideal for photography from vehicles; this image of a red grouse was one such result.

500mm lens; ISO 125; 1/200 sec at f/4

Understanding Exposure

Exposure is a combination of lens aperture, camera shutter speed, and sensor speed. Such a mix may sound complicated, but there are a few simple ground rules that when followed should ensure successful exposure for each shot.

What is a correct exposure? In effect, it is recording the bird in the way that you want, ensuring that detail is retained in the brightest and darkest areas. There are three things working in conjunction with each other that determine the exposure you use. They are the camera's shutter speed, lens aperture, and sensor sensitivity—expressed as an ISO value.

You will hear photographers talking in "stops" when discussing exposure—a stop is simply the term used to describe an increment, whether it is increasing or decreasing the amount of light being let through a lens.

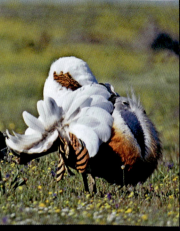

ABOVE This displaying great bustard needed plenty of depth of field and a fast shutter speed to freeze the bird's quivering movement.

500mm lens; ISO 100; 1/500 sec at ƒ/8

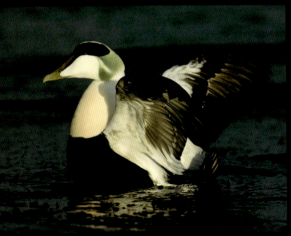

LEFT Eiders are a favorite subject of mine. This common eider drake was photographed in northern England in the spring. When photographing birds with white tones in the plumage, take care to ensure detail is not blown.

500mm lens; ISO 100; 1/800 sec at ƒ/5.6

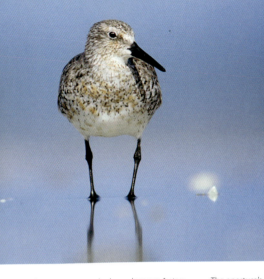

LEFT This image of a red knot was taken on a beach in Florida during the middle of the day. The surroundings were very bright, so to gain an accurate exposure quickly I used the spot-metering mode—taking a reading off the bird's breast. I also used an angled viewfinder on the camera.

500mm lens; ISO 100; 1/1000 sec at *f*/8

The apertures marked on a lens are *f*-stop numbers and, on a lens of short focal length, typically range from *f*/2.8 to *f*/32. At *f*/2.8, the aperture on the lens is wide open, allowing the maximum amount of light to the camera's sensor, while at *f*/32 the lens aperture has just a small opening, letting little light in. When we want to let more light in, we use the term "opening up." When we want to decrease the amount of light coming in, the term is "stopping down."

Each increase or decrease in the range either doubles or halves the amount of light being let through to your camera's sensor. For a lens with a typically large *f*-stop of *f*/2.8, the series would be *f*/2.8, *f*/4, *f*/5.6, *f*/8, *f*/11, *f*/16, *f*/22, *f*/32. These are standard one-stop increments. Moving up the scale, you halve the amount of light traveling through the lens by adjusting the size of the hole—or aperture.

The aperture's role in the creativity of a photograph is to control the depth of field. This is the area in focus from the nearest to the farthest point in the picture. At *f*/2.8, the depth of field is very shallow, whereas at *f*/22 the background to the subject is likely to be in reasonable focus.

The shutter in your camera normally opens for a fraction of a second, and as with *f*-stops, it either halves or doubles the amount of light hitting the camera's sensor depending on which way you go with the scale. However, most cameras and lenses allow you to measure not in whole stops but, if you so desire, in increments of one third of a stop. Typical camera shutter speeds range from thirty seconds or longer to 1/4000 sec or even 1/8000 sec.

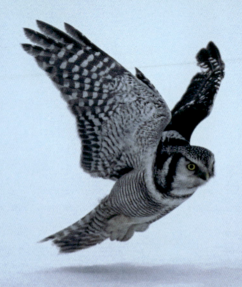

The ISO value is the final piece in the exposure jigsaw. ISO stands for International Standards Organization and traditionally describes film speeds, although a DSLR dictates the speed of your sensor. Typical DSLRs range from ISO 100 to 3200: the higher the rating, the more sensitive the sensor is to light. Higher ISO settings mean that less light is needed to make a picture, enabling images to be taken in poor light conditions, or with higher shutter speeds and smaller apertures.

The ISO rating you choose acts as the basis for your exposure. Higher ISO values in DSLRs come with drawbacks in the form of increased signal noise. Although not the same as "grain" in film, this has a similar effect in that the image is degraded. Signal noise

ABOVE Hawk owls fly extremely fast, so a fast shutter speed is required to freeze them in midflight. On the day I took this image the light was very poor; so that to gain a shutter speed of 1/2000 sec I had to use a high ISO of 400.

500mm lens; ISO 400; 1/2000 sec at ƒ/4

RIGHT For this image of a red-throated loon, I had to choose a fast enough shutter speed to freeze the action, but I also needed a large enough depth of field to make sure that the head and some of the body was kept in focus.

500mm lens; ISO 320; 1/500 sec at ƒ/8

normally starts to become apparent with ISO values of 400 and above. Having said this, there are some DSLRs that exhibit little signal noise at higher ISO settings, so this may not be an issue for you—experiment with your camera and see how it fares. Of course, in poor light a picture may only be possible with a high ISO, but to keep quality as high as possible, an ISO of between 100 and 200 is recommended in most situations.

Once your ISO value is set, the shutter speed and aperture are linked. Alter the value of one, and the value of the other has to be changed to provide a correct exposure. There is only ever one correct exposure, but many different combinations of shutter speed and aperture; this is known as "exposure ratio." If, for example, your camera's meter tells you the correct exposure is 1/250 sec at ƒ/8, and you decide you need a faster shutter speed of 1/500 sec, then by halving the amount of light coming into the lens to retain the correct

exposure, the aperture needs to be opened up one stop to ƒ/5.6, thus allowing the same amount of light to hit your camera's sensor. Creating a picture is a balancing act of choosing the right aperture for the effect you want along with a high enough or low enough shutter speed.

On a typical DSLR there are three light-metering options to choose from. Matrix or multipattern metering takes information from across the picture to give a reading and is the most sophisticated of the three. It is fooled occasionally, but for much of the time it is very accurate. My preferred option is center-weighted metering, which takes a central area of the frame usually defined by a square or circle visible in the camera's viewfinder. Finally, there is spot metering, which is useful for evaluating an exposure in a small area of the image but should not be used all the time, as readings will vary wildly within the picture depending on where you point the camera.

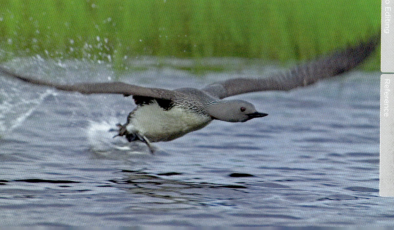

Exposure and Histograms

The histogram function is one of the digital camera's greatest advantages over film, allowing you to check for over- or underexposure on the spot and then correct it, without having to wait for a film to come back from the lab.

The histogram displayed on the back of your camera is your primary tool for nailing a correct exposure. Ignore this and your exposures are likely to be wayward, leading to poor image quality.

It is tempting to use your camera's LCD screen image to visually assess whether your photograph will look right. This is a big mistake; for a start, the screen's brightness can be adjusted, and viewing conditions may also be far from ideal. Use the screen for looking at composition, and to roughly check

sharpness, but do not rely on your screen for assessing exposure.

A DSLR's histogram maps out the brightness levels in an image, from black on the left to white on the right. The vertical axis shows the number of pixels for each level. In a well-exposed image, the range of brightness levels stretches across the histogram. If the histogram is bunched to the left, it is likely the image is underexposed, and if leaning to the right it may be overexposed.

Use the histogram to check that you are not clipping data at either end. Specular highlights, such as the sun or highly reflective surfaces can create a spike tight against the highlight end of the histogram. These cannot be helped, but blowing highlights that contain important details—such as in white plumage

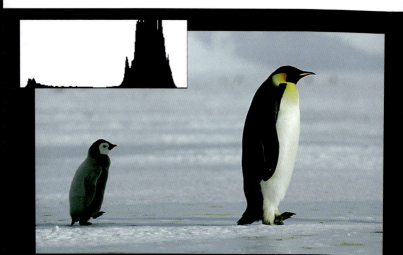

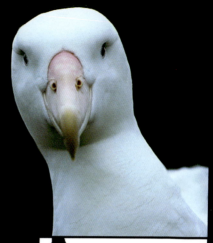

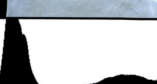

LEFT In this image of an emperor penguin with chick, the snow, ice, and white breast of the penguin are represented by the majority of pixels being bunched to the right-hand side but not clipped. You can see the dark back and head of the penguin represented by the "mini mountain range" on the left. Care needs to be taken with pictures such as this to make sure your histogram shows no, or very little, clipping.

100mm lens; ISO 100; 1/500 sec at f/5.6

ABOVE Histograms can, of course, take on many different shapes. In this example there are mainly dark and light tones with just a few midtones, so the pixels are bunched at either end. I have gone for as correct an exposure as possible here, exposing the whites of the wandering albatross just about perfectly without clipping. I could have underexposed the whites to be safe, but this might have introduced distracting signal noise to the dark background.

500mm lens; ISO 100; 1/125 sec at f/11

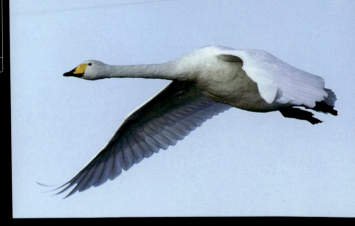

or snow, must be avoided, as these details cannot be retrieved in Photoshop. On these occasions it is better to slightly underexpose for whites, which at least can be restored.

Underexposing an image too much leads to noise (similar to grain in traditional photography) in dark and shadow areas, so it is important to expose as accurately as possible. A full exposure, or one that tips toward overexposure, will retain better detail, as more data is retained in highlights than in shadows; however, again care must be taken not to blow the highlights. The best way of checking for this, apart from just viewing the histogram, is to use the blinker function on your camera. This causes all the blown highlights to flash in the picture when viewed on the camera's LCD.

ABOVE LEFT The histogram for this flying whooper swan clearly shows the predominance of light tones, of both the sky and white plumage of the bird, by the pixels being grouped toward the right. Be careful that the peaks shown at the extreme edges of a histogram are not "clipped," or cut in half, as these images will probably show lost detail in the brightest or darkest areas.

500 mm lens, ISO 200, 1/500 sec at f/6.3

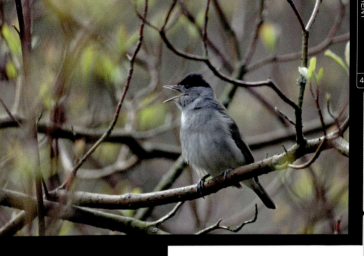

ABOVE RIGHT This correctly exposed image of a singing blackcap has many midtones within the image, so the majority of the pixels are in the middle of the histogram.

500mm lens; ISO 100; 1/500 sec at *f*/5.6

To sum up, it is better to have your histogram leaning toward the right but not clipped, rather than being bunched up to the left. However, if your subject and surroundings have a lot of light tones, take care not to blow highlights and if necessary underexpose a little to retain detail. You can always rescue detail from underexposed parts of an image if not clipped, but never from blown highlights.

Histograms and your LCD can be difficult to see in bright conditions on some camera models, but you can buy specially adapted bellows to help with viewing. However, I can recommend a free alternative—a cardboard toilet-roll tube is ideal.

Freezing Action

Some of the most exciting and dramatic images of birds are taken when they are in motion—flying, diving, swimming, and so on. Being able to capture this action means using fast shutter speeds while retaining some depth of field.

Birds are, by their very nature, highly active creatures, and they are rarely still, whether they are feeding, fighting, courting, or flying. Capturing action, therefore, is a big part of bird photography. Digital cameras provide a good deal more opportunity for freezing motion in comparison to their old film counterparts. The higher sensitivity of a digital sensor compared to film means we can use faster shutter speeds to capture stills of behavior not seen before, since this style of working only existed in the limited domain of the high-speed specialist.

It is easy to underestimate the shutter speed required to freeze all movement in a small flying bird such as a wader. The bird might be flying at 30–40 mph and flapping its wings at a fast rate—such movement can normally need at least 1/1000 sec to avoid blur, and even then the wing tips might suffer. Generally, the smaller the bird, the faster the shutter speed required to freeze movement.

A few years ago I had the opportunity to photograph a hunting hawk owl, which would appear in a tree above snow-covered pastures, as it looked for movement above or below the snow, largely preying on field voles. On occasions when it flew close, its speed of flight was breathtaking, and I found that to freeze all movement I had to use 1/2000 sec; for many of the images I took I used 1/4000 sec to ensure the wing tips were pin sharp.

RIGHT White-throated dippers fly at more than 30 mph (50 km/h), so freezing such a small bird in flight becomes a big challenge. I have failed to freeze the wing tips even when using a shutter speed of 1/1000 sec. However, in this case, having slightly blurry wings adds to the image by encouraging a feeling of movement.

300mm lens; ISO 400; 1/1000 sec at *f*/4

BELOW A hovering kestrel on the look out for prey requires a fast shutter speed to stop the rapid wing movement from blurring the image. To help I increased the ISO to 160.

500mm lens; ISO 160; 1/750 sec at *f*/8

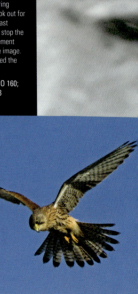

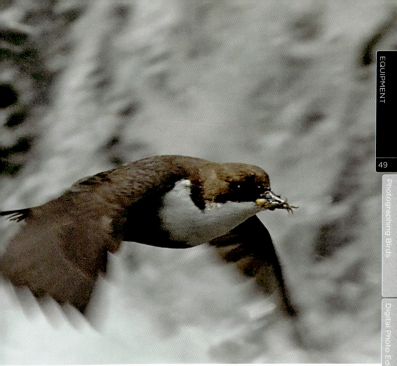

When shooting action, you want the fastest shutter speed possible, but this may mean having to use a wide aperture and shallow depth of field. This can be quite a dilemma, but even slow shutter speeds, such as 1/60 sec, can freeze a wing stretch if you take enough images. Basically, this will always be a balancing act; keep in mind it is often better to have the key parts of a bird in focus and risk movement rather than having an out-of-focus element distracting from your pin-sharp subject.

Useful action photography relies on you having some knowledge of your subject and being able to anticipate behavior. It is likely that for most opportunities you will be using a long focal-length lens; getting used to handling and adjusting controls without having to take your eye from the viewfinder takes practice, but is essential if you are not to miss out on some potentially great shots. Autofocus comes into its own when tracking a running, swimming, or flying bird, and when things start to happen, take as many shots as possible. Keep an eye on your buffer—it is important when shooting with lower-priced DSLRs, which have fewer frames per second and longer image-processing times, that you don't shoot too early, lock the camera up, and miss the peak of the action.

Motion Blur

Blurring motion using slow shutter speeds can give dramatic effects. Trial and error will show the most appropriate speeds for a particular type of motion or action, but there are some rules to follow in order to maintain image quality.

Blurring motion has become somewhat *de rigueur* for wildlife photographers in recent years, since it is a great way of illustrating movement. Motion-blur images also have their detractors. For some people such pictures leave them cold, while for others a motion-blur image can be regarded as a real piece of art.

Motion blur brings a whole new dimension to bird photography in my view; with this technique pictures can resemble paintings, creating a mood and atmosphere in an image that may be lacking if the bird's motion had been frozen. Whenever I am shooting birds in flight or running, I am always assessing whether there is potential for motion blur to enhance the picture.

One of my favorite subjects is flamingos, which, because of their colorful plumage, provide excellent subjects for slow shutter speeds. On East Africa's Rift Valley lakes, lesser flamingos parade in groups up and down the shoreline in a courtship ritual that involves the shaking of heads and fast walking. The image below was taken on the shores of Lake Nakuru, and to enhance the movement I used a shutter speed of 1/15 sec—any slower and the movement may have been too much, making the birds indistinguishable; any faster and too many sharp components may have been visible in the picture, so losing the effect.

This illustrates how unpredictable capturing motion-blur images is—the effect you will get cannot be gauged in advance. To hedge your bets when taking a sequence, take as many images as possible, and if the action is repeating itself regularly, as with the flamingos opposite, you can experiment with shutter speeds. I find that speeds between 1/8 sec and 1/30 sec work best, with around 1/15 sec giving the most consistent results.

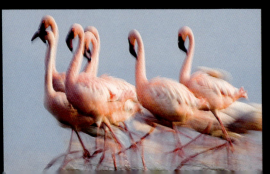

LEFT A group of lesser flamingos rushes along the shore of Lake Nakuru in Kenya's Rift Valley. Although I took many conventional shots of this scene, those where motion blur was introduced by using a slow shutter speed have worked best.

500mm lens with angled viewfinder; ISO 100; 1/20 sec at *f*/32

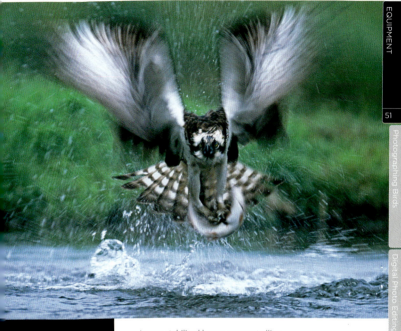

Photographing Birds

Digital Photo Editing

Reference

ABOVE This osprey exploding from the water in Finland with a trout grasped in its talons is one of my best-known motion-blur images. I used a beanbag laid on top of the lens to help keep the shot stable.

300mm lens; ISO 100; 1/15 sec at _f_/16

Image-stabilized lenses are great allies when shooting motion-blur images, since they help eliminate a lot of the camera shake that may be inevitable when using long lenses at such slow shutter speeds. These lenses help restrict the blur to the faster-moving parts of the bird. In many instances, having some sharpness to the bird's head, or at least its eye region, is desirable; if you have a very blurred head, a lot of the impact and focus of the photograph can be lost. A Wimberley tripod head (see page 37) is also useful, as it allows for a steady, smooth panning action, helping to eliminate shake from the lens.

Understanding Depth of Field

Accurate control of depth of field is a crucial element in creating the pictures you desire. The depth-of-field preview button, a standard feature on quality digital SLR cameras, allows you to check and adjust the depth of the field before actually taking your photograph.

The depth of field in an image is defined as the area in focus from the nearest to farthest point, and it is controlled by the lens aperture. Being able to control depth of field in your image is one of your most important tools for creating the photograph's mood. For example, with a 300mm lens wide open at *f*/2.8, the depth of field will be very shallow, isolating the bird from its background. The same frame photographed at *f*/22 will have a far greater depth of field, and the background may be clearly visible. In short, the higher the *f*-stop, the greater the depth of field.

At any chosen aperture, the farther your subject is from the camera the more your depth of field increases; therefore, when birds are very close you need to check that you have enough depth of field for the entire bird to be sharp, if this is what you desire. You do this by using a depth-of-field preview button on your camera. This tool is indispensable when choosing a DSLR, since without one you will not be able to judge with any accuracy where your nearest and farthest points of focus are.

Most bird photographers aim to shoot with the lens as wide open as possible as this allows for as fast a shutter speed as possible, but, more importantly when using a long telephoto lens, it also creates a pleasingly out-of-focus foreground and background, thus placing attention on the bird. This is particularly helpful when birds are set against very messy or distracting backgrounds.

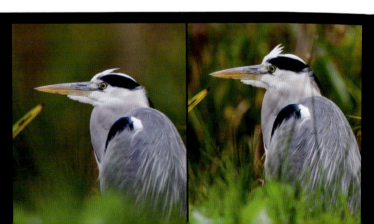

Using a shallow depth of field on birds close up can offer opportunities for high-impact images. The eye is nearly always going to be the focal point in an image for a viewer, so you should always aim to at least have this sharp. There will be occasions when a large depth of field can give a real feel of sense of place, providing the viewer an opportunity to gaze upon the surrounding habitat in which the bird is placed.

Focusing on more than one bird can present you with a dilemma: do you go for maximum depth of field and try and get both birds? If you are focusing on a flock, do you try to get as many as possible sharp, or do you selectively focus on an individual and push the rest out of focus? If the birds are too close to put them cleanly out of focus, it is often best to try for a large depth of field and get as many as possible in focus, as birds that are just out of sharp focus can be very distracting.

LEFT These two images of a gray heron's head illustrate how a background can be controlled by choosing an aperture to give more or less depth of field. The first image was taken with an aperture of ƒ/4; this very shallow depth of field throws the messy background into a soft wash of color so attention can focus on the bird. The second image was taken with a large depth of field—ƒ/16 in this case—which creates a more untidy background and foreground.

BELOW I purposely wanted a large depth of field for this image of a soaring bald eagle, in order to illustrate the bird's habitat by showing the snow-capped mountains in the bottom of the frame.

300mm lens; ISO 100; 1/250 sec at ƒ/16

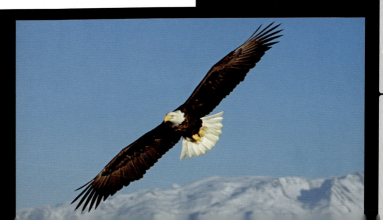

Memory Cards

The capacity of memory cards is increasing on a regular basis. However, with 10 megapixels now commonplace in compact cameras and 14+ megapixels in DSLRs, combined with an increasing number of photographers shooting Raw, file sizes are now bigger than ever.

A memory card is the card your camera uses to store the images it processes. The card is removed when full, and the images can be transferred from card to computer using a USB card reader, the direct cable connection supplied with your camera, or inserted directly into a printer for instant prints.

There are a variety of card formats, but the three most commonly used are Secure Digital (SD)—including mini and micro SD, SDHC, and SDXC—and various Memory Sticks and CompactFlash (CF) cards. As a general rule of thumb, compact cameras, including the more recent compact interchangeable lens cameras, tend to use the smaller SD format, DSLRs utilize the larger CF cards, while memory sticks are primarily used in Sony cameras. However many cameras will also take more than one type of card.

Cards come with varying storage capacities, normally ranging from a few hundred megabytes (Mb) to up to 16, 32 and even 64 gigabytes (Gb). If you are a digiscoper shooting relatively small-sized JPEGs, you will only need to use small-capacity cards. The higher the capacity, the more expensive they will be.

If you are a DSLR user and likely to be shooting in the Raw format (see page 58), you will be able to fit far fewer pictures onto a card, so consider buying a high-capacity one. I currently use 4Gb cards, which take around 200 images when shooting in Raw; if shooting in basic JPEG mode, the same card could take around 2,000 images—a big difference!

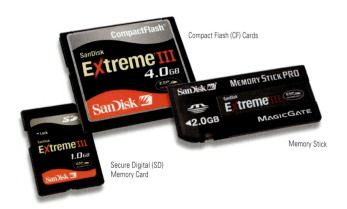

Compact Flash (CF) Cards

Memory Stick

Secure Digital (SD) Memory Card

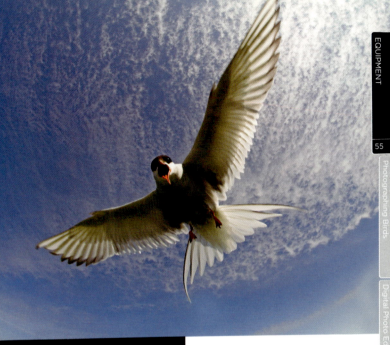

LEFT Memory cards come in various guises. The two most important considerations are the capacity, which dictates how many images you can fit on the card, and the write speed. The faster the write speed the less likely the camera will lock when shooting a sequence of images.

ABOVE When shooting action sequences such as with this arctic tern mobbing me on the Farne Islands, cards with high write speeds ensure that your images are accepted onto the card from your camera's buffer quickly, thus avoiding the camera locking due to a full buffer.

10.5mm lens; ISO 200; 1/1000 sec at ƒ/11

Another point worth considering when choosing cards is their varying write speeds. The write speed is the speed at which the card receives and stores the information being fed to it by your camera. The faster the write speed, the quicker your camera's buffer will clear, and, in theory, the more shots you can fire off during any one opportunity.

Finally, there will come a time when you will actually wipe a card before downloading the pictures from it—this has happened to the best of us, but unlike when you spoil film by opening the back of a film camera before rewinding, there are various ways of retrieving the information—a quick search on the Internet will reveal some recovery options.

File Formats

There are two broad categories of file format, compressed and uncompressed. All interchangeable lens cameras including compact and DSLRs offer both types, but only some fixed lens compacts.

The compressed format that all digital cameras utilize is called the JPEG (pronounced "jay-peg"). JPEG stands for the Joint Photographic Experts Group, which designed the format, and is a compression method used to store images at a much smaller size. The JPEG is known as a "lossy" format because the data is squeezed into a small space so that some is lost in doing so. With a JPEG image, not all the color information your camera is capable of capturing will be kept, although this loss may arguably not be readily apparent to the human eye.

Every time you make adjustments to a JPEG and resave it, you lose information; this accumulates so that over time deterioration in the image will be evident. JPEGs can be taken at a variety of quality settings depending on your particular make of camera, but usually from basic to fine. When shooting in the JPEG format, you set certain parameters in your camera, such as the level of sharpening, white balance, saturation, and so on, and these parameters are applied to the image.

If your camera only shoots JPEGs, and you want the best image quality, always select the finest setting.

Of the two uncompressed formats commonly used today the Raw format is more widely used. Raw images are, as the name suggests, images with no parameters set. Although the parameters you set in your camera will be attached to the picture file, they do not have to be applied and can be modified in Raw processing software, downloaded to the computer at a later stage during post-processing. For example, it's possible to alter the White Balance setting from say "Sunny" to "Cloudy" without any deterioration in image quality (see page 135).

Some camera manufacturers, aware that some photographers may want the quality and flexibility of Raw files, but still keep file sizes down, offer smaller resolution Raw formats, such as sRaw. Additionally, an increasing number of cameras allow photographers to shoot both Raw and JPEG at the same time. That way you have the benefit of "ready to print" JPEGs with a Raw file should you wish to undertake more in-depth post production work. This option, though, does use up a lot of memory space.

The other common uncompressed format is the TIFF. TIFF stands for Tagged Image File Format and is only available on some DSLRs. When shooting TIFF files take far longer to be processed by your camera than Raw files, and they also take up more space on memory cards, so there is little reason to shoot TIFFs. However, TIFFs are commonly used in the digital imaging workflow when Raw files are converted during post-production for processing and outputting.

RIGHT Close-up of four shots of the same bird, processed to emulate the effect of increasing compression. Even at this relatively high magnification the difference between them is quite subtle, however, the larger image files (least compression) show smoother tonal gradation. JPEG compression works by analyzing and coding pixels in groups of 64—these secondary mosaics of 8x8 pixel squares begin to become more noticeable the greater the level of compression.

TIFF

FINE

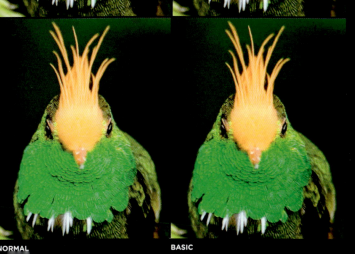

NORMAL

BASIC

Which Format—Raw or JPEG?

Many authors have debated the pros and cons of shooting JPEGs as opposed to Raw images. My advice is that if you have the ability on your camera to shoot Raw images, and your aim is to produce the best-quality image you can, then there is no debate: you should shoot in Raw format.

If you cannot avoid shooting JPEGs, make sure you are using the best-quality setting, usually defined as "JPEG fine." Lower settings will definitely affect the quality of your picture. Some of the advantages of JPEGs include being able to store many more images on a memory card compared with the much larger Raw files, the little work needed to be done to images once out of the camera, and finally, all photo-editing software readily reads JPEG images, whereas Raw images may need special plug-in software to read the files from certain camera models.

As mentioned above, if your camera gives you the ability to shoot in Raw, the benefits are soon realized:

- Color information can be lost from a JPEG file, but a Raw file, if processed well and converted to an RGB TIFF, will be superior. Having said this, depending on your final use, this superiority may not be immediately noticeable.
- A Raw image gives complete freedom to experiment with white balance, exposure, and various other parameters.
- Every time you make an adjustment to a JPEG and then resave it, you are slowly degrading the image, although this will not be very noticeable if only done on a few occasions.
- Processing Raw images for the first time may seem like a daunting task, but it is soon easily mastered (see page 134).

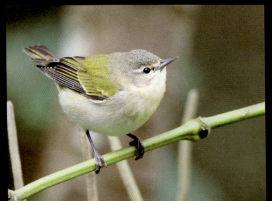

LEFT I came across this Tennessee warbler late in the afternoon when the low sun was creating a warm glow. I did not want the warbler's plumage to be rendered too warm, but I did not have the opportunity to experiment with white balance in the camera. However, because I was shooting in Raw, I was able to adjust the white balance at the editing stage, re-creating the true colors of the warbler's plumage.

500mm; ISO 200; 1/50 sec at f/4

Raw files and image editing

A digital camera Raw file is a copy of all the data captured by the camera's sensor in a single exposure, without the camera having compressed or manipulated that data in any way. This violet-bellied hummingbird was photographed in Raw format (left), which meant I could remove the blue cast without loss of detail. The result is on the right.

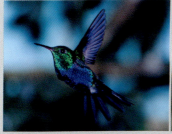 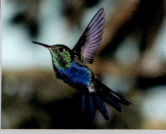

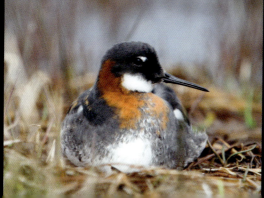

LEFT I poorly exposed this image of a female red-necked phalarope, but because I had shot the image in Raw, I was able to recover the subtle colors without too much damage to image quality.

70–200mm zoom; ISO 100; 1/320 sec at *f*/5.6

Taking Care of Equipment

Dust is the greatest enemy of digital cameras, and by shooting outdoors and in all seasons, you are also likely to encounter rain, snow, and hail. There are ways to protect and clean cameras, but you have to work very carefully and thoroughly.

The very nature of bird photography means that equipment takes a beating from the elements—whether it is getting covered in salt spray, dust, or being rained or snowed on. Thankfully, there are a variety of useful measures we can take to offer protection and clean our gear.

Dust is the big enemy: digital sensors are prone to attracting dust particles due to the charge they create, so changing lenses in dusty environments should be avoided unless absolutely necessary. To check how dusty your sensor is, take an image of the sky with the lens stopped down to, say, f/16 or f/22. The dust will show up, particularly if you view the image at a hundred percent on your computer screen. Some of these dust particles are too small to matter. Larger particles will appear on your pictures, and these will need to be cloned out: this can be time-consuming, so it is sensible to keep the sensor clean.

How you clean your sensor is really down to personal preference. I hold my camera in the air, with the front facing downward, open the shutter by putting the shutter speed on the bulb (B) setting, and then squirt air by hand using a Giotto bulb blower. Holding the camera up so that the front is facing down

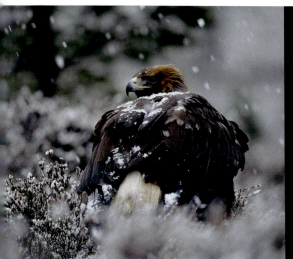

LEFT Heavy snow makes for very evocative images of winter. I was well-sheltered from the weather to get this shot of a Scottish golden eagle, and I had a lens bag over my lens for protection.

500mm lens; ISO 200; 1/250 sec at f/11

ABOVE RIGHT Photographing this parasitic jaeger was a challenge due to gale-force winds blowing sand over my gear and me. Although there is a risk of getting sand or dust inside your camera in such conditions, you certainly should make the most of adverse weather. This would have been an ordinary portrait without the blowing sand.

500mm lens; ISO 400; 1/500 sec at f/8

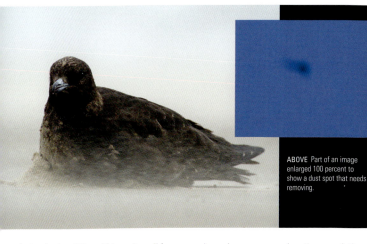

ABOVE Part of an image enlarged 100 percent to show a dust spot that needs removing.

helps the dust fall out. This works well for me and keeps my sensor clean. Some experts discourage this technique, however, suggesting dust might be pushed into inaccessible nooks and crannies.

The alternative is to use a swab kit and/or special brushes that use an electrostatic charge to pick up the particles. A variety of these can be found for sale on the Internet, but they can be very expensive, ranging from a few dollars to many hundreds. I would suggest never using compressed air, as there is always the danger of moisture being squirted onto the sensor, which might then be very difficult to remove. If you have stubborn marks, you can get your camera manufacturer to clean the sensor. Nikon and Canon offer this service for a fee.

I have a friend who persists in using his shirt to clean his lens. This practice is not recommended! When you take a close look at the end of his lens, it looks like people have been ice-skating on the glass! Whenever you clean a lens, use proper lens tissue or cloth. These can be bought cheaply at optometrists and are relatively inexpensive, compared to replacing the lens front element.

Bad weather, such as snow or even heavy rain, can lead to some interesting opportunities with birds and can transform a run-of-the-mill portrait into an eye-catching one. When the weather does turn bad, you need to protect your gear so you can continue shooting. You can use a large plastic bag, but these do rustle and blow around in the wind; it is far better to purchase custom-made lens covers, which are available from a number of sources, or you can make your own—shower caps are a good idea for protecting the camera in rain or snow.

PHOTOGRAPHING BIRDS

One of the questions I get asked most is, where can I go to get good pictures? The easy answer is that there are opportunities all around you. You don't have to jet off to exotic locations or jump in your vehicle and travel to a bird reserve—if you have a backyard or a local park, these are great places to start, both to hone your skills and to practice your field craft.

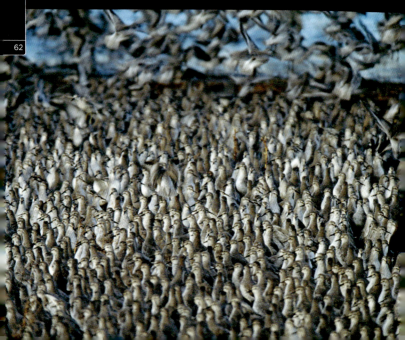

When my interest in bird photography started, I was a teenager with no transportation other than a bicycle. So for years I would set off from home armed with my camera and attempt to photograph the birds local to me. I got to know my patch very well, and I knew the opportunities available at different times of the year. I often failed, but on those days I managed a successful stalk and got what I considered a good picture, it made the pleasure all the sweeter, due to the many disappointments I experienced.

Above all, this apprenticeship taught me good field craft. I developed the ability to read how close a bird would allow me to approach, I became expert in predicting behavior, and I perfected my stalking technique. There is no substitute for experience—good field craft is not learned from a book such as this. Although I can give you plenty of tips, you need to get out   and learn from your

mistakes. Concentrating on your local birds is the best way to start.

The next few pages give an overview on how to tackle some birds common to a variety of habitats, and this is followed by suggestions for utilizing creative techniques.

When my pictures started being published in the mid-1980s, good bird photographs were those considered to be well-lit portraits, sharp flight shots, and attractive images of birds at the nest. Now, equipment has improved to the point where the parameters of what makes a great bird photograph are continually moving, and there are new opportunities for capturing pictures showing rarely seen behavior and action. Although action pictures are currently the new vogue, there is so much more to making a good image than capturing a fleeting moment: direction of light and perspective will always be key elements to creating a strong picture.

OPPOSITE The sense of movement and mass in this picture of red knots creates an arresting image.

RIGHT Silhouette images can emphasize the elegant lines of a bird, giving a striking picture.

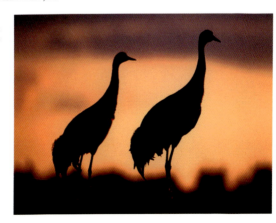

Backyard Birds

There is no better way to start taking photographs of birds than by practicing on the ones closest to you in your backyard or some other neighborhood locality. Tempt the birds to spend regular time in your yard, and you'll get great photo opportunities.

Some years ago I started feeding the birds at my local nature reserve, and before long I had hordes of birds queuing up to jump on the feeders. After using portable canvas blinds for a couple of years, I went upscale and had a converted wooden shed installed. You could utilize your garden shed, if placed in a reasonable position for the light: open the

window and place camouflage netting across, and you have a ready-made blind.

You might be able to shoot from your kitchen window; if your regular backyard birds are used to people in the house, you might not even need to be concealed. I don't need to use the blind for some species at my feeding station, as some of the blue tits are so tame they perch just inches away when I am filling up the feeders. If your backyard birds are tame, this is a big bonus when it comes to photography. But remember if you are not concealed, the shier species will stay away.

When setting up a feeding station in your

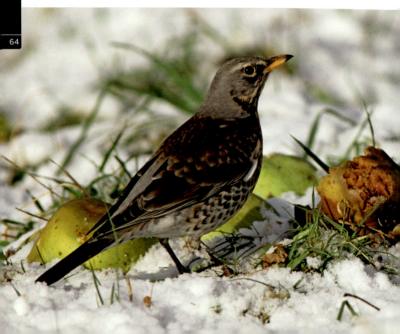

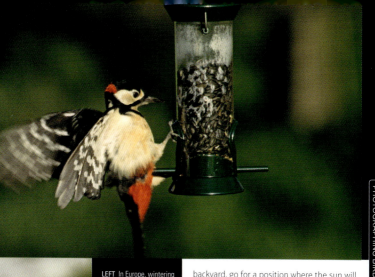

LEFT In Europe, wintering thrushes readily come to apples put out in the backyard. This fieldfare was a regular visitor for a few cold weeks one January, making an easy and attractive subject to photo while feeding.

500mm lens; ISO 100; 1/250 sec at f/11

ABOVE Don't automatically ignore images of birds on feeders. Although luring a bird onto a decent-looking perch makes for an attractive photograph, some dynamic images can be taken of action on and around the food source, such as this image of a great spotted woodpecker.

300mm lens; ISO 100; 1/500 sec at f/5.6

backyard, go for a position where the sun will be behind you during the part of the day you intend to be photographing and match this with a good, clean background. If good backgrounds are hard to come by, you can easily manipulate this by placing a subtly colored cloth or board to act as an out-of-focus backdrop. I have two I use regularly; one painted in a pale blue wash to mimic the sky, the other in a nice soft shade of green. The great thing about backyard photography as opposed to stalking birds in the wild, is that you can control the background lighting and available perches.

In my experience, the key to attracting lots of birds is to put out as much food as you can afford and to provide as big a variety of food as possible. For example, I may have up to ten feeders, a bird table, and food sprinkled on the ground when not taking pictures. The advantage of attracting big numbers is that when you come to photograph you can remove nearly all your feeders: this creates a queuing system, meaning birds have to perch around the feeders before there is space to jump on.

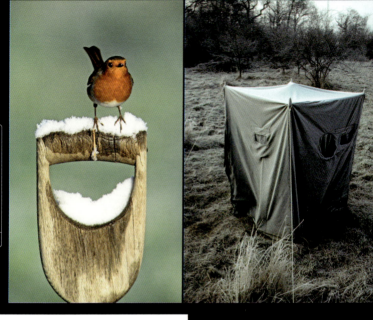

A variety of foods is key to attracting a good variety of species. In the United States, foods can range from sugar solutions for hummingbirds, fruit for tanagers and orioles (the latter like oranges sliced in two), mealworms for various species including bluebirds, and peanut butter smeared on logs and tree trunks for woodpeckers. Various seed mixes can be bought to attract specific species. Put niger seed out, and you are soon likely to have a regular flock of goldfinches; peanuts are excellent for tits and that common garden visitor, the great spotted woodpecker, while apples and pears are a big hit with thrushes.

ABOVE LEFT Garden implements can be used as perches when illustrating birds in the garden, adding an extra dimension. This robin readily perches on a fork handle due to hidden bait.

500mm lens; ISO 100; 1/500 sec at ƒ/8

ABOVE Canvas blinds can often be very useful when photographing birds in the backyard.

RIGHT A white-crowned sparrow was lured into view by placing mixed seed below the bush.

500mm lens; ISO 100; 1/640 sec at ƒ/5.6

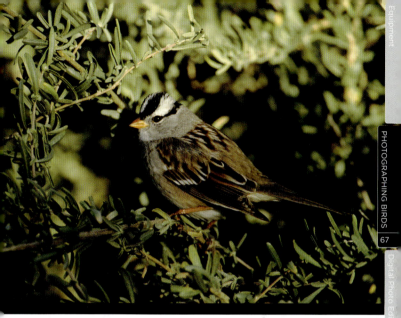

The chances are that you will not want your pictures to feature the garden feeder that the birds are visiting, so the trick here is to place a decent-looking perch close to the feeder but not too close so that it appears in the picture. The birds will then use the perch before jumping onto the feeder or bird table to feed. Perches can really enhance the picture—I often spend long periods of time looking for suitable twigs, branches, logs, and sometimes rocks to use. If you snap a twig, make sure the break does not show, or if unavoidable, smear some mud over the break to disguise it. There are all sorts of tricks you can use to get birds to use perches: for example, I regularly photograph robins on all sorts of garden implements, luring them onto fork handles, flowerpots, and even a garden gnome! I do this simply by placing mealworms in an old film canister and taping it to the perch just out of shot.

Food is not the only way of attracting birds—they need water too, and a small pond or simply a receptacle with a drip will work. A perch can be placed out of sight of your receptacle, or if birds are coming to a small pond, you can line the banks with moss or other attractive natural features to hide any signs of the pond being man-made.

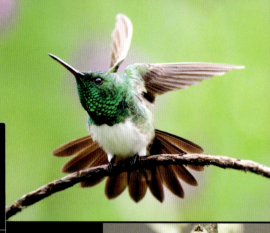

LEFT This beautiful snowy-bellied hummingbird was photographed in the gardens of a lodge in Panama, South America. Because this hummer was coming back to rest on the same perch after each feeding foray, I was able to tidy up the background, eliminating a cluster of tiny branches that would have distracted from the beauty of the bird.

500mm lens; ISO 200; 1/125 sec at f/5.6

RIGHT If you have an attractive tree or shrub in your garden, simply place food close by and photograph the birds as they arrive and leave. I placed bananas on a bird table below this bare branch to attract this golden-hooded tanager to perch.

500mm lens; ISO 125; 1/500 sec at f/5.6

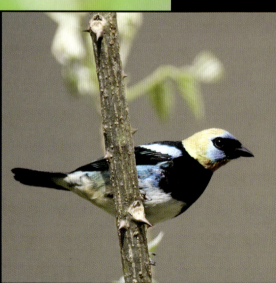

Pro tip

If you have a good-sized backyard, it is worth planting shrubs that produce berries and other plants attractive to birds. A well-placed mountain-ash tree or other tree that bears berries or fruit will provide great photo opportunities for a variety of species during fall and winter. If you plant native shrubs or trees, your pictures will look all the more authentic.

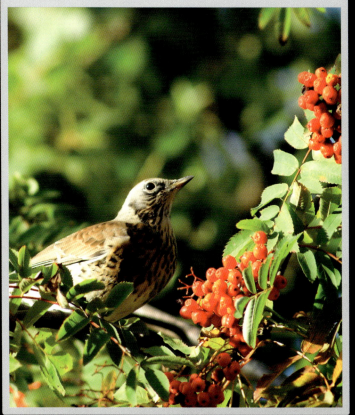

Urban Environments

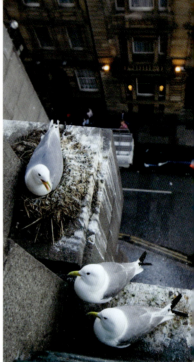

Many species of bird have become familiar sights in cities and towns, and they offer chances for eye-catching images. In addition to obvious places, such as parks and public gardens, keep an eye out for nesting and roosting places on buildings.

Towns and cities may not readily spring to mind as great places to photograph birds, yet where birds come into close contact with people and are not harmed, they readily become tame. Town and city parks are the obvious places to visit within urban environments, offering green spaces where a range of species can feed, breed, and roost.

In central London, England, St. James's Park can be outstanding for bird photography, for example. One of the attractions here, as with many parks all over the world, is a lake that attracts a range of wildfowl; these waterbirds are fed daily by hordes of people, and so are easily approached. When visiting parks, I like to take my own food and move away from other people so I can control the birds more easily. Often the earlier you visit in the day the better, not just because of the light, but because once lots of people start appearing, the slightly more timid birds will become harder to approach, and lots of people throwing food out can make your quest to manipulate your subject's position very difficult.

Apart from the obvious waterfowl attractions of park lakes, any areas of woodland and shrubbery also yield results. Large areas of grass attract thrushes and other lawn-loving species to feed, particularly if lawn sprinklers are on.

Away from these green oases, many other opportunities exist, particularly for making images that portray birds living in the urban environment: I lived in the city of Newcastle in

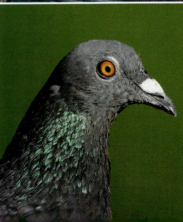

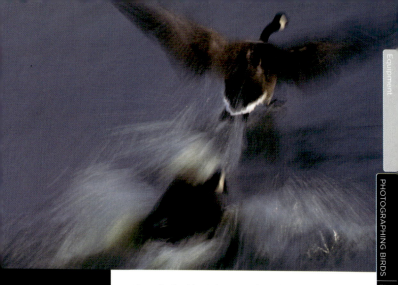

LEFT TOP Towns and cities can be surprisingly good places for bird photography. These black-legged kittiwakes are nesting on building ledges in the center of Newcastle, England.

17–35mm zoom; ISO 200; 1/160 sec at f/5.6

LEFT BOTTOM Familiar birds, such as feral pigeons, are likely to be very tame and thus offer good opportunities for close-ups.

200mm lens; ISO 200; 1/500 sec at f/5.6

ABOVE This motion-blur image of squabbling Canada geese was taken in St. James's Park in the centre of London.

300mm lens; ISO 100; 1/15 sec at f/16

northeast England for eighteen months and found a number of opportunities for doing just this. One of the big natural attractions in Newcastle is the kittiwakes that nest on the buildings close to the river, in the heart of the city. They are so used to people coming and going when roosting on their chosen nest ledges that I was able to get close enough to use a wide-angle lens, portraying the birds within the context of their urban environment.

Botanical gardens can be productive sites, particularly as they are often in urbanized areas that offer a refuge for many species. Kew Gardens in London is one such place where a host of woodland species can easily be approached: pheasants strut through carpets of bluebells in spring, while the wooded areas are favored by species such as wood pigeons that are difficult to approach in the countryside.

Seabirds

Whether seen in flight behind a boat, diving after prey, nestling in colonies, or feeding their young, seabirds are always fascinating subjects, and if you can incorporate their environment into an image, so much the better.

Seabird colonies offer endless opportunities for bird photography. In the northern hemisphere, most colonies are alive with frenetic action from mid-May. North America has some special sites, not least the often fog-shrouded Pribilof Islands. Britain and Ireland play host to some of the most spectacular colonies in the world, too; the combination of sea cliffs bordered by the rich North Sea and North Atlantic means millions of seabirds make their home there.

The sheer number of birds at close proximity, the sounds—and sometimes the smell, too—is what makes a visit to a seabird colony so unforgettable. A full range of lenses will come in handy here: wide-angles can be used to shoot colonies on dramatic sea cliffs, for example, and there can often be very tame birds that can be used as foregrounds to a wider scenic shot. This is a really popular image with British photographers when photographing Atlantic puffins, which can be hand-tame—indeed, I have had puffins playfully tugging at my laces while sitting on a cliff top!

Apart from images of static birds, flight shots should come thick and fast in many colonies, as birds come and go from their fishing grounds. Wind direction can play an important part in how successful you are with this, since the wind will determine in what direction to the light the birds arrive and

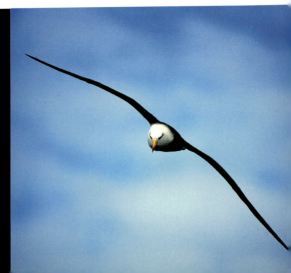

RIGHT Many species of seabird follow boats, and a trip to Antarctica by boat is a great way to photograph albatrosses. This black-browed albatross was photographed from the stern of a ship, handholding my lens.

500mm lens; ISO 100; 1/1000 sec at f/5.6

FAR RIGHT The tiny least auklets swim ashore by the millions in the North Pacific. This pair was on St. Paul Island in Alaska's Pribilofs.

500mm lens; ISO 400; 1/160 sec at f/8; fill-in flash set to -3 depart from the colony. This is because seabirds, much like any other species of bird, will whenever possible take off and land into the wind.

With the majority of species, photography is often best toward the latter half of the breeding season when birds are returning with food for their young. For those that do not nest down in holes or in crevices, there will be the rearing of chicks to photograph, offering interesting images of the interaction between parents and young.

Two things to bear in mind when photographing seabirds at a colony; first, avoid any undue disturbance—this is particularly true around tern and gull colonies, which should be avoided unless they can be photographed from a vehicle or custom-built blind. Secondly, take great care on cliffs: it is very easy to get wrapped up in taking pictures and lose all caution—accidents do happen!

Seabirds away from colonies are a different proposition altogether. If you join a cruise to Antarctica, great opportunities can be had from the ship photographing the albatrosses, petrels, and other birds that follow the boat. Closer to home, car ferries can be excellent for shooting images of gulls.

Seabirds on the wing offer a big challenge, particularly in a rocking boat. At many locations, pelagic trips are offered to view and photograph seabirds; perhaps the most outstanding can be found in New Zealand off Kaikoura, or California's Monterey. The ideal lens is usually a 300 or 400mm lens coupled with a converter. The lighter and shorter the lens, the easier it is to follow birds while on a rocking boat.

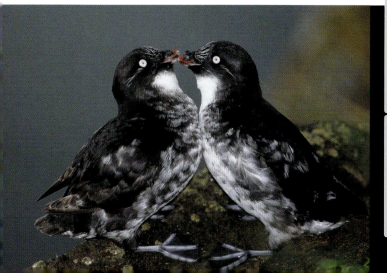

Wildfowl and other Waterbirds

Unlike small birds, which require a close approach for a pleasing image, wildfowl, and families such as storks and herons, offer a variety of approaches, since these are big birds that reside in usually very open and sometimes very scenic habitats. As with seabird photography, a range of lenses can be employed to photograph them.

Big flocks are a feature of wintering wildfowl and allow plenty of artistic interpretation. Goose flocks sometimes explode into the air, and post- or preroost flocks can often be silhouetted against a warm, orange sky.

How easy it is to stalk waterfowl depends very much on the location and can vary dramatically at different locations in the same region. This is due to many species being hunted, and where this happens, approaching them may be impossible. At refuges, however, where they are left alone, some species become very tame.

Many species give signs of imminent action—for example, whooper swans communicate by bobbing their heads before they take off, while many species of duck will shake their heads or also bob. As you gain experience, you will learn these various signs, which give you a warning to be ready with your finger on the button. Birds will always take off into the wind if they need a running start to become airborne, so by placing yourself on the flight path for takeoff, you can maximize your chances of getting a good action sequence.

Divers, grebes, and diving ducks can all be stalked by using a simple method of moving closer only once the bird has dived; each time it emerges, freeze, and don't move until it dives again. Another way of getting close to waterfowl on the water is to utilize a floating blind; these are becoming increasingly popular, and if you are reasonably good at DIY they are easily constructed. I used one for a few years, which enabled me to capture some really eye-catching, low-level images of ducks and swans, as they took little notice of the blind.

Herons, egrets, and spoonbills nest in colonies, and close approach can be made without risk of disturbance at some locations. Famous rookeries for photography include Bharatpur in northern India, one of the world's great wetlands where thousands of breeding waterbirds put on a spectacular show. At the other extreme is the Venice rookery in Florida, which consists of a small island in a small lake that hosts breeding great blue herons and great egrets. Despite this smaller scale, the photography here is no less spectacular.

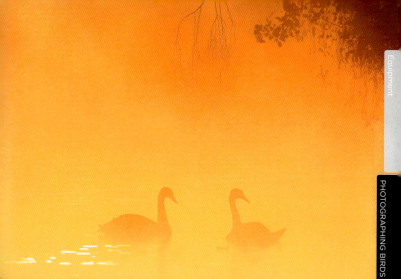

LEFT This horned grebe was tricky to approach, but by moving only when the bird was diving, I was able to creep close enough.

500mm lens; ISO 400; 1/250 sec at ƒ/5.6

ABOVE These mute swans were captured a minute or two after sunrise. Within ten minutes, the mist had burned off.

300mm lens; ISO 100; 1/500 sec at ƒ/11

RIGHT The snow geese and Ross's geese in New Mexico's Bosque Del Apache Reserve offer the bird photographer a photographic feast.

500mm lens; ISO 100; 1/500 sec at ƒ/8

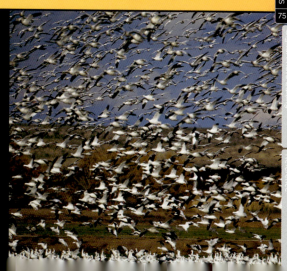

Birds of Prey

With their incredible eyesight and extraordinary patience when locating and catching their prey, raptors are among the most spectacular of all birds. They are also among the most wary, making them a true challenge to photograph.

Attempting to photograph birds of prey in the wild offers a big challenge. This is why many of the pictures you see published are of captive raptors, often passed off as being in the wild (see page 86 for more on this). All species can be photographed given time, patience, and knowledge.

There are now a number of opportunities available at baited sites. Baiting—that is the putting out of food—is very effective in attracting species ranging from golden eagles to red kites and even ospreys. This is a far more attractive proposition than attempting to photograph at the nest, where many species may easily be disturbed. Indeed, it is a criminal offense to photograph a number of species at the nest without the relevant licenses.

Because of the birds' shy nature, if you are baiting a site you will need to use a blind. Raptors have incredibly good eyes and may sit out of sight of your blind for many hours, watching the bait and looking for anything suspicious before coming down to feed. This is especially true of golden eagles—I once watched a golden eagle from my blind in Finland for seven hours before it finally flew down. It is thus imperative not to create any suspicion when in the blind, this means leaving your lens alone—have it trained on the bait, but don't start moving it around for no reason—and if you have to move, do it very slowly. With golden eagles, if I have a bird on bait I may take two minutes or more to move the lens just a few inches. You might think this is overkill, but once the birds sense danger they will go, and they may never come back.

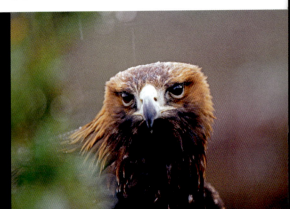

RIGHT I have spent many enjoyable hours photographing ospreys. This shot was taken from a pylon blind (a blind on stilts) overlooking a nest in Finland. The female was brooding her young during torrential rain.

500mm lens; ISO 100; 1/250 sec at f/4

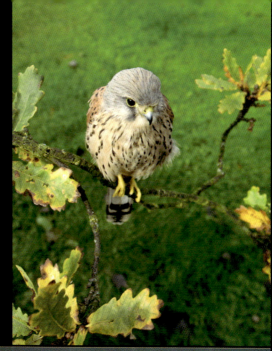

RIGHT I shot this kestrel from above to present an unusual perspective. A shallow depth of field concentrates the viewer's attention on the bird.

300mm lens, ISO 200, 1/250 sec at *f*/5.61/125 sec at *f*/5.6

BELOW Golden eagles are extremely suspicious, so great care needs to be taken when photographing them and other raptor species from blinds at baited sites.

500mm lens; ISO 400; 1/125 sec at *f*/5.6

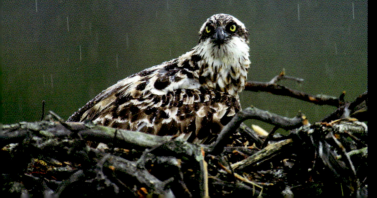

Because raptors can sit concealed while watching a baiting site, it is often best to arrive at your blind in the dark if you are on your own, and leave in the dark, too. If you have a friend or two who can walk to the blind with you and leave once you are inside, then it is probably OK to do this in daylight, as the birds will be fooled into thinking any danger has left.

Not every species will need such measures, of course. There are some opportunities that are commercially run for photographers, with everything, including the birds, arranged! These include the sight of sea eagles in Norway, which are thrown fish from boats in the fjords—great action images can be taken on these trips. In Britain, Gigrin Farm in Wales is well known among bird photographers as the place to photograph red kites. Here the farmer feeds the birds on lumps of meat and fat thrown out in front of a row of blinds at exactly the same time each day. The birds know when to arrive, and over a hundred kites may be present, performing a stunning aerial ballet in front of rows of telephoto lenses.

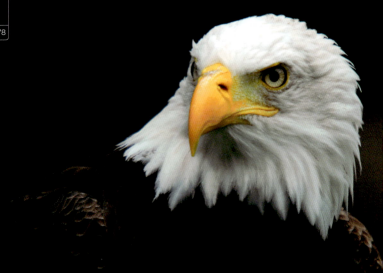

Perhaps the ultimate baited site I have visited is in Finland, where close to Tampere is a fish farm that attracts a constant stream of ospreys. Here the fish farmer has turned the marauding birds into a benefit by creating a sandy-bottomed pool that has been packed full of fish he cannot sell at market. The birds fish constantly in the pool as it is so easy, and with the provision of photographic blinds the opportunities are spectacular. Away from baited sites opportunities can be had at migration points, for example in Gibraltar, and in the U.S., at Cape May in New Jersey.

BELOW The African fish eagle is indigenous to Africa, where it is found near bodies of water in most of sub-Saharan Africa. It is an ancient form of sea eagle. To capture this type of fast-moving action shot, you may need to increase the ISO setting in order to get a sufficiently fast shutter speed in order to freeze the movement.

500mm lens; ISO 200; 1/500 sec at ƒ/4

LEFT The bald eagle, the national symbol of the United States, is a type of sea eagle. It feeds by snatching fish—it's most important source of live food—from near the surface of the body of water using its powerful talons.

500mm lens; ISO 100; 1/250 sec at ƒ/4

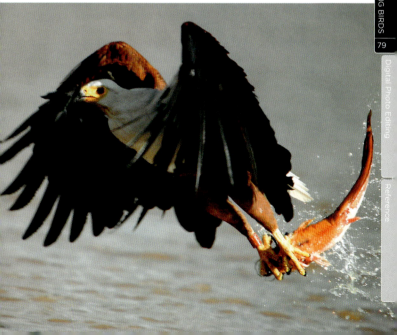

Game Birds, Crakes, and Rails

In addition to taking photographs of game birds in fields and in flight, there are regular opportunities to capture images of lekking, where large groups of male birds display in an attempt to entice females.

Game-bird photography is most popular in spring when some species congregate at leks, the communal display grounds at which the males display in an attempt to attract females to mate—in North America, prairie chickens strut their stuff, while in Europe both capercaillie and black grouse are the two big draws for bird photographers.

Lekking of most grouse species occurs early in the morning and can often be over soon after dawn, which presents the fundamental problem of available light. I have experienced many frustrating mornings in blinds photographing capercaillie, witnessing fantastic behavior prior to dawn, and then,

once there was enough available light to photograph, the lek fizzling out and the males dispersing. Such experiences are common, which means it is best to try and make multiple visits. Due to the shy nature of most grouse and the danger of disturbance at a lek, you need to be in the blind while it is still dark. While capercaillie leks are often deep in pine forests, black grouse leks tend to be more in the open and will normally go on longer into the morning, so photography at these is less of a challenge.

In some years, "rogue" capercaillie are found in both Scotland and Scandinavia; these are males that are completely unafraid of humans and will indeed attack. They are so pumped up that they display to anyone who approaches—they make great photo subjects, but beware when around them, as you can end up receiving a nasty peck.

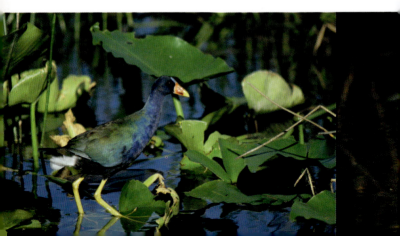

BELOW LEFT This American purple gallinule seemed oblivious to a long row of enthusiastic photographers lined up on the Anhinga Trail in Florida's Everglades.

300mm lens; ISO 100; 1/500 sec at f/8

BELOW RIGHT This is a male rogue capercaillie photographed in early spring in Finland. Rogue capercaillie offer great photo opportunities due to their fearless nature—but beware, they often attack!

300mm lens; ISO 100; 1/250 sec at f/11

BELOW Water rails, in common with many species of crakes and rails, are normally very shy, but they can be enticed to a regular spot with bait. I used peanuts to entice this bird into the open.

500mm lens; ISO 400; 1/250 sec at f/5.6

Away from the breeding season, game birds, particularly pheasants and partridges, can be attracted to bait. Corn spread on the edge of fields or on woodland boundaries may entice red-legged and gray partridges, as well as the ubiquitous pheasant. Crakes and rails can be enticed into the open with bait, too. I have photographed sora rails coming to mealworms, and other water rails can be baited with casters (maggot chrysalis), peanuts, and a more natural food, hawthorn berries. During the breeding season, many species will respond to tape playback, although this of course needs to be used judiciously, and within the law.

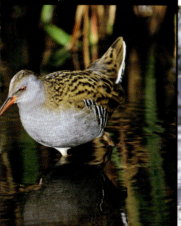

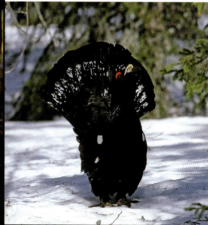

Shorebirds

Migrant shorebirds can travel thousands of miles each year, so those you photograph may have come from the other side of the world; on the same shoreline you can also see "local" birds, whose whole lives are spent there.

Shorebirds are a big favorite for many bird photographers. Many species undertake remarkable migrations of many thousands of miles, while others are more sedentary in their habits. The approachability of many shorebirds is very dependent on location in the world, so very different techniques need to be employed, depending on how your birds react to people.

In North America, many shorebirds are very tame: Jamaica Bay in New York State, for example, is a popular spot for photographing migrant waders in the fall. Here a close approach can be made to most species, so stalking techniques can be used. One of the reasons for their approachability here in the fall is that many may not have seen a human before, having been born just a few weeks earlier. Contrast this with Europe, where many waders do not tolerate human approach: clearly stalking can be out of the question here. To take the knot as an example, in Florida and other sites in the United States, you can often approach this species on foot to within a few feet, while in Great Britain it is likely that a knot will take flight once you are within two or three hundred feet at best. Many bird reserves in Europe have good blinds suited to shorebird photography. The alternative to those on reserves is to use your own blind.

Each fall I erect a blind at my local reservoir on a pool where water levels are controlled just for the birds' benefit. The gradual growing expanse of mud as fall progresses attracts migrant waders such as common and green sandpipers, greenshank, snipe, and sometimes rarer visitors. I set my blind up for the early morning light, so the sun rises just to one side of it before moving around the back; this gives me a well-lit scene for a few hours. I have the blind set for early mornings so that I can arrive and enter it in the dark: this way I don't arrive, scare everything away, and have to wait a long time for all the birds to return.

Alternative sites for shorebird photography include coastal sites where there are regular roosts. If you know of a popular roost site, you can set up your blind and wait for the birds to arrive at high tide. Some roost sites can be spectacular—more than 100,000 birds can be present, creating a photographic feast as they wheel around in vast, tightly packed flocks.

Pro tip

Where shorebirds share beaches or harbors with people, they are often far more approachable than those feeding far out on mudflats. It is always worth investigating busier beaches for this reason. If you spot shorebirds feeding along the tide line, watch which way they are moving and sit down ahead of them. Chances are, if you are still, they will come close enough for a picture.

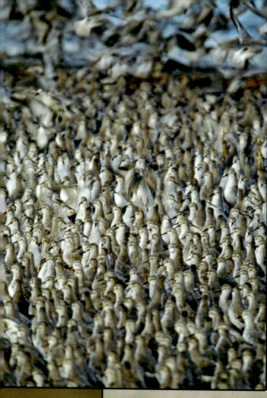

LEFT During fall and winter it is worth visiting shorebird roosts. These red knots are gathered at the famous high tide roost at Snettisham on the Wash in southeast England. This shot was taken from the public blind.

500mm lens; ISO 200; 1/250 sec at f/4

BELOW LEFT Some species of shorebird, such as this Eurasian golden plover in Scotland, are easier to photograph during the breeding season, when they also look their best.

500mm lens; ISO 100; 1/250 sec at f/8

BELOW RIGHT A few shorebird species gather at lekking sites in spring to attract a mate. Some spectacular action can take place in these avian arenas, such as these male ruffs in combat.

500mm lens; ISO 200; 1/1000 sec at f/4

Equipment
Digital Photo Editing
Reference

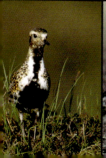

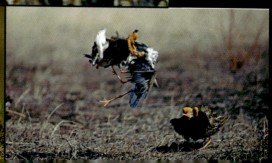

Passerines

Passerines, or small perching birds, are the most frequent visitors to backyards, but their size and tendency to perch deep in a tree or hedge makes them difficult to photograph. There are, however, a few methods for luring them out.

As a general rule, the smaller the bird, the faster it moves, and the more difficult it can be to photograph. The warblers are a good example of a family that require plenty of field craft to obtain good images. Apart from the problems of getting close and having to use long lenses, the added challenge when photographing small passerine species is to create pleasing images within their often cluttered habitat of twigs, branches, and messy backgrounds.

Getting a good background is often just down to perseverance, but also be aware of what a difference moving an inch or two can make with a long lens. In addition, by using a shallow depth of field with a long lens, even the most cluttered of backgrounds can be transformed into a pleasing backdrop.

Stalking passerines can be a big challenge, and it is far better to try luring the birds to you. We have already discussed backyard feeding stations, but don't restrict your feeding just to the backyard. Water is the other big magnet for birds since most need to drink and bathe regularly to keep their feathers in good shape. In hot locations, a drinking pool should not take long to start working; a simple saucer or upturned garbage-can lid sunk into the earth and then filled with water will do, and by placing a perch close by, you are immediately in business. In North America, photographers have found that water drips work really well for attracting a range of species, particularly warblers—simply suspend a water receptacle above a pool or dish and let it slowly drip from a small hole in its base. The species and country you are photographing in will dictate whether a blind is necessary.

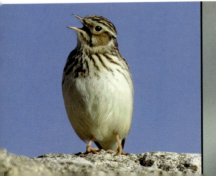
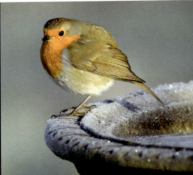

BELOW FAR LEFT Driving down a mountain road in Greece with the window open one morning, I heard a woodlark singing. I eventually located the bird on a boulder. By recording its song and then playing a quick burst back to the bird, the woodlark was soon singing on a boulder right by my car.

500mm lens; ISO 160; 1/750 sec at ƒ/8

BELOW LEFT This robin visits my garden birdbath regularly to both drink and bathe. I took this image to illustrate the robin in the garden; however, if you want more natural-looking shots, you can easily make a small drinking pool and landscape it to look natural.

300 mm lens, ISO 160, 1/250 sec at ƒ/5.6

BELOW Most birds need to drink and bathe regularly. Hawfinches commonly come to drinking pools.

500mm lens; ISO 160; 1/500 sec at ƒ/5.6

BELOW RIGHT Warblers present the photographer with a big challenge, as their fast and erratic movement, often through heavy cover, means perseverance is often needed. They are easier to photograph at migration watch-points in spring and fall. This paddyfield warbler was photographed on the Isles of Scilly in England one October, where there was little cover to hide away in.

500mm lens; ISO 100 with fill-in flash; 1/125 sec at ƒ/8

The other commonly used method for luring songbirds in particular is to use tape playback in spring, either by playing a prerecorded song or recording the song of a singing male and playing it back. For some photographers this is unacceptable, but I have no qualms about using playback in a limited way. Where it should not be done is at sites where birdwatchers use the technique regularly to see certain birds, as the constant stream of visitors playing songs at a particular site can have a detrimental effect on a bird's well-being— if the bird does not respond within one or two plays, it should be left alone.

There are plenty of recordings available, and you can use an MP3 player or a small CD player with speakers to transport around in the field. I prefer to playback a bird's own song, as this normally evokes a stronger response. To be really accurate with where you want the bird to land, you can place a speaker next to the perch.

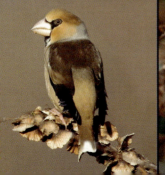

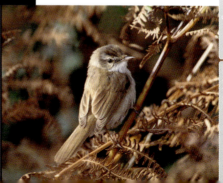

Captive Birds in Natural Surroundings

If photographing a wild bird, particularly a bird of prey, in its natural habitat is not an option, it is possible to find captive birds in special centers. Falconers own raptors, and they will often work with photographers to create natural-looking shots.

Working with captive birds can open up all sorts of creative possibilities difficult to repeat with individuals. All the keen photographers I know photograph captive birds—for many of us, the chance of photographing a wild golden eagle, for example, is one that is never going to happen (unless we invest an enormous amount of time and have the miraculous opportunity and access). The trick to photographing captive birds, whether they be ducks in a wildfowl collection or raptors owned by a falconer, is to make them look wild.

Much care and attention is needed to execute this type of bird photography properly. If you are photographing birds of prey with a falconer, then arrive at the location at least an hour early. Scout it out, look for suitable perches, and think about light direction, backgrounds, and opportunities for getting creative with different angles. If you take the time to know exactly where you want to place the birds and the type of shots you want from the session, you will have a much better chance of success.

If the raptor you are shooting has jesses on, try to conceal them by placing that leg behind the other, or perhaps place some foliage in front. I sometimes use out-of-focus foregrounds to disguise the legs of a bird, either by shooting at a low angle along the ground or placing an object close to the lens in the line of focus. You can clone out telltale signs that the bird is captive, though this can be very time-consuming and often tricky.

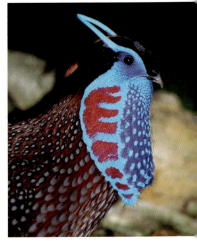

The other popular captive subject for bird photographers in Great Britain is wildfowl. When shooting this subject, the one thing to remember is to conceal the pinioned wing by photographing the bird on its "best side."

Occasionally opportunities present themselves in zoos or other captive collections. When shooting through netting or bars, ensure you hold your lens flush up against the wire to prevent the picture from being soft or showing evidence of the bars. If there is a cage in the background, try to disguise this by using a shallow depth of field to help throw it out of focus.

It is good practice to declare that a photograph is of a captive bird; this is particularly important if you have your work published—and if you enter competitions, you will certainly have to.

LEFT Just because they cannot escape does not mean that captive subjects are any easier to photograph than subjects in the wild. This Temminck's tragopan lived in a large enclosure. Only by sitting quietly in one corner for a couple of hours was I able to take this image of a male in his full display.

500mm lens; ISO 200; 1/250 sec at ƒ/5.6

RIGHT Some great opportunities are offered by wildfowl collections. Here, a male red-breasted merganser is displaying in early spring.

500mm lens; ISO 100; 1/500 sec at ƒ/4

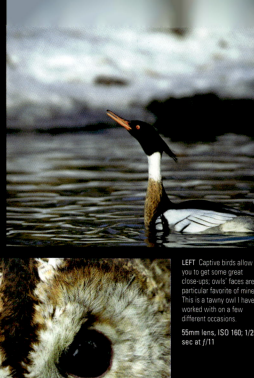

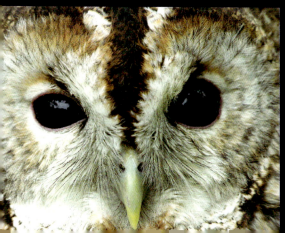

LEFT Captive birds allow you to get some great close-ups; owls' faces are a particular favorite of mine. This is a tawny owl I have worked with on a few different occasions.

55mm lens, ISO 160; 1/250 sec at ƒ/11

Birds in Flight

Shooting birds in flight is one of the bird photographer's biggest challenges. getting the best results requires a combination of good positioning, forward planning, and a thorough knowledge of your camera's autofocus controls.

The biggest hurdle to overcome when taking good flight shots is finding the opportunity to be in the right position. Regular flight paths that provide opportunities include bodies of water where wildfowl will be taking off, such as on the edge of a tern colony or perhaps on a migration route. By carefully identifying such locations, good opportunities will come your way.

Whenever I am out with my camera, I am on the lookout for unexpected flight shots. Some of my best images have come from spotting a bird heading toward me and then being ready to take advantage of the situation very quickly. Using quick-release plates on lenses will help you speed up when whipping your lens off a tripod.

Autofocus will have no problem locking onto birds against clear backgrounds, such as blue sky or water, but problems can arise when you track a bird against a landscape—if your autofocus point wanders off the bird, it may easily lock onto the background, so that suddenly you are struggling to lock the focus

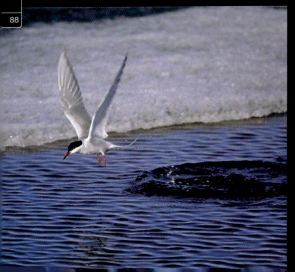

LEFT Flight shots do not always have to be frame-fillers: I wanted to include the ice and the splash from this common tern's fishing success, so I used a shorter lens.

300mm lens; ISO 200; 1/1750 sec at *f*/8

back on again. When this happens, take your finger off the shutter button and depress again once the bird is in the viewfinder—by keeping the shutter button depressed, the autofocus might start hunting and the opportunity will be lost.

I normally use the middle autofocus sensor for tracking flying birds, and on a big bird I try to focus on the neck or head so that the eye will be sharp. By focusing on the body when firing the shutter, it is possible to lock onto the wing on the downstroke; if you are using a shallow depth of field, the head of the bird will be out of focus—of course, this is easier said than done!

Because of their low contrast, white birds can cause autofocus systems to hunt. There is no easy answer to this, other than using a combination of autofocus and manual focusing if your lens allows. Sometimes I resort to focusing manually on a preset point and shooting a burst of images as I see the bird coming into focus in the viewfinder. This normally captures at least one sharp image.

Flight photography is best attempted with lightweight 300mm and 400mm lenses; however, I do hand-hold my 500mm lens regularly. The key requirement is to use a fast enough shutter speed, at least 1/500 sec.

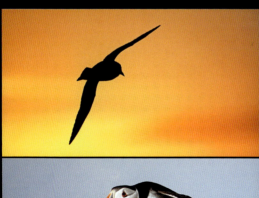

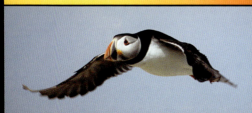

LEFT Just as with composing a static bird, try and place a flying bird in the frame for a pleasing composition. I was able to place this silhouetted cape petrel close to the top of the picture, giving the effect that it was flying into space.

500mm lens; ISO 50; 1/500 sec at ƒ/5.6

LEFT BELOW Seabird colonies are good places for flight shots. I deliberately selected a slow shutter speed in order to blur this Atlantic puffin's wings for artistic effect.

500mm lens handheld; ISO 100; 1/1000 sec at ƒ/8

Shooting Low

The best bird photography narrows the gap between the human and avian world, revealing bird life as other birds might see it. Angling shots of birds at their level goes a good way toward this, and the results are often worthwhile.

If you compare an image taken at a bird's-eye level with one taken looking down from a fully extended tripod, there is no contest as to which will look best. Eye-level images create an intimacy between bird and viewer, thus having greater impact, while an image taken from above looking down on a bird usually gives a sense of detachment.

Of course I am not suggesting that shooting low-level images is the only way to photograph birds, but a low level does create more pleasing images than a higher viewpoint: out-of-focus foregrounds and backgrounds become soft washes of color, which helps to throw emphasis onto the bird.

Your neck will be badly cricked if you attempt to look through the viewfinder when laying on the ground. The best solution is to use a waist-level or angled viewfinder that attaches to the eyepiece of your camera. I normally mount my camera on my tripod with its legs fully splayed or alternatively rest the lens on a beanbag. On occasion, I just rest the lens on the ground using the lens mounting foot, though this setup is not particularly stable. If you don't want to lie on the ground, by using a long lens and standing back, the angle of view will be shallower. Start to move in closer to a bird while standing with a long lens, and you will notice that the viewing angle becomes more acute.

Wildfowl are a good subject for shooting really low. If you can find a park lake that has a footpath on the same level as the water, laying down and shooting the birds from this position can give the effect of being in the water with them.

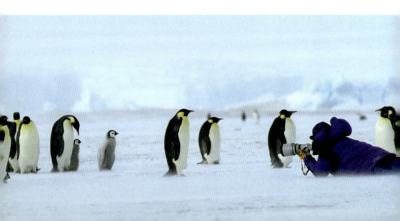

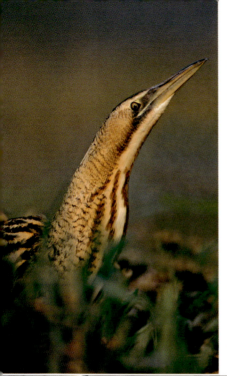

Pro tip

It is easy to lose a sense of the horizon when shooting low and thus end up with a great shot except for an obvious tilt in the background. Always check the horizon position behind your subject, and if you find the terrain a problem in this way, try using a small spirit level. These are available from some camera stores and can be stuck in an appropriate place on your camera.

FAR LEFT Photographing an emperor penguin at its level.

LEFT I was able to approach this bittern in a shallow-bottomed boat. By laying down, I managed this intimate view as it peered at me from between the reeds.

500mm lens; ISO 100; 1/350 sec at *f*/4

BELOW This image shows lesser flamingos feeding—the low angle helps to reinforce the sense of a maze of legs. Taken at Lake Nakuru in Kenya's Rift Valley.

500mm lens; ISO 200; 1/400 sec at *f*/11

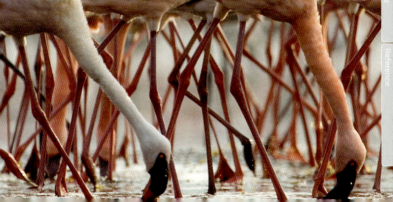

Lighting

Unlike studio or still-life photography, when photographing birds you have to work with the light available to you and your subject. That said, there are a number of methods that will gain you a measure of lighting control.

The quality and direction of light falling on a bird will have a dramatic impact on the mood created in the image. The best light of the day generally occurs in the couple of hours after the sun rises or before the sun sets, as the golden glow of the sun low in the sky helps to enrich colors. However, on bright,

overcast, or cloudy days, I have no qualms about taking pictures throughout the course of the day. Even on bright, sunny days, if a good opportunity for an image arises, I take it.

Although midday light can be harsh, this is not a reason to pack the camera away. Fill-in flash can help soften harsh shadows, and Photoshop can be used to easily create catchlights in eyes when post-processing. Having said all this, as soon as my shadow becomes shorter than me when the sun is shining, I do ease off a little until the light improves later in the day.

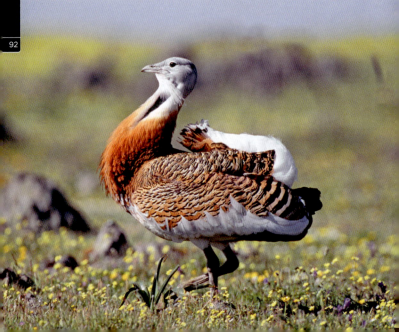

Pro tip

When photographing birds with iridescent feathers, you want to be able to bring out these colors. Watch a hummingbird, and you will see flashes of color, depending on how the light hits the bird's plumage. Normally, to capture these colors on film, you need to be straight on to the bird as it faces you. Using a flash can help. This stunning picture of a male rufous-crested Coquette hummingbird was photographed in Panama, and for the most part showed a black throat and breast. Only when it turned toward me did I see this beautiful emerald green display. I used fill flash to help in showing this off.

LEFT Strutting across the Extremaduran Steppe in Spain, this great bustard is beautifully front-lit, helping to bring out the rich colors of the male's plumage.

500mm lens; ISO 100; 1/500 sec at ƒ/8

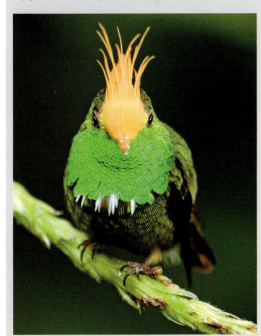

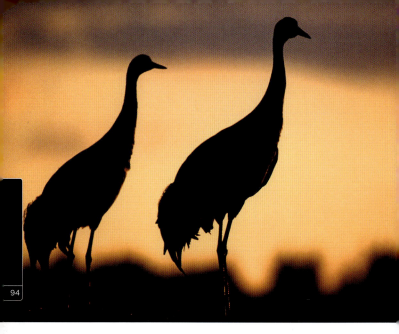

There is always a temptation to shoot nicely front-lit bird images: colors are always rendered well, there are few shadows created, and many pleasing images are created in this way. For shots like this, you need to ensure the sun is shining from over your shoulder. However, I would urge you to experiment with the direction of light, since more eye-catching images can be made by bucking the trend. While front-lit images are two-dimensional in appearance, you can create more perceived depth in an image when there is a three-dimensional look. To achieve this, you have to use the direction of the light to create contrast with shadow.

The other lighting options are sidelighting and backlighting. Sidelit images can look dramatic, elevating a pleasing portrait to something more striking. Sidelighting works best when the sun is low—this kind of shot is not so effective in the middle of the day—and I also find that shooting low helps. You should ensure that the lit side of the bird is correctly exposed, because if any areas are burned out the effect is lost; by exposing for the lit side, the shadows will take care of themselves. Sidelighting can give a three-dimensional look to an image that is particularly effective with large birds.

Backlighting can be dramatic, too; the mood of a picture shot from the front can be completely altered by shooting in the opposite direction, but watch out for lens flare caused by internal reflections from lens elements. Chipped or scratched glass or dirt on the lens can also cause problems; to avoid this use a deep lens hood, or try shading the top of the lens with your hand. When using

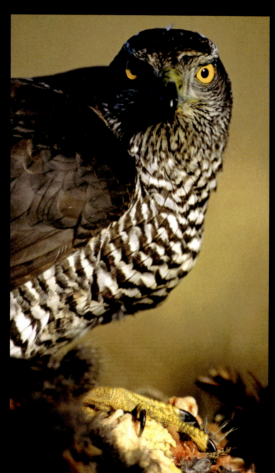

LEFT One of my favorite silhouette images, this pair of common cranes are about to depart for an overnight roost on Lake Hornborga in Sweden. They walked to the top of the rise just above my blind before taking off into the air.

500mm lens; ISO 100; 1/250 sec at ƒ/4

RIGHT The sidelighting on this northern goshawk helps accentuate the feeling of a ruthless predator, adding a mood that might have been missed if conventionally lit.

500mm lens; ISO 100; 1/250 sec at ƒ/5.6

backlight you can achieve a wonderful rim-lighting effect if your subject is against a dark background—the outline of the bird becomes lit up, as if wearing a halo.

Silhouettes can be produced through strong backlighting, aligning your bird in line with the setting or rising sun, or at least against a bright, colorful sky. Bird silhouettes work best when the outline is easily recognizable. Examples might be a cormorant drying its wings, a crane silhouetted in flight, or perhaps an eagle.

Good silhouette shots are rarely unexpected; they take a bit of planning and knowledge of favored perches or flight opportunities. It is then a matter of waiting for the right conditions and hoping the bird cooperates by using the chosen perch.

To what degree you silhouette your subject is personal choice, often any exposure to within two or three stops will work, the variance being the intensity of the colors in the sky. You can control this in Photoshop and, if shooting in Raw, in the camera's Raw converter. I tend to expose for an area of sky that is close to the sun but does not contain the brightest part and then use this as a base reading. You can experiment, but remember that when your histogram has the silhouetted bird in the frame, it will show tall spikes on

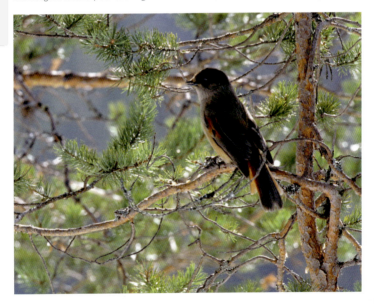

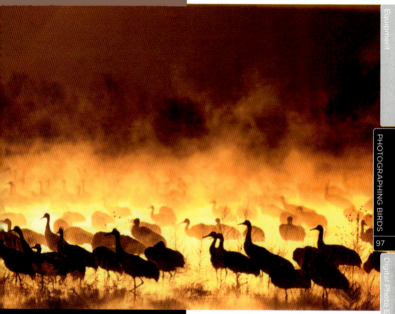

LEFT Snow is an excellent reflector, and reflected light can help to create some wonderful images. Look how the pine needles and Siberian jay are beautifully backlit, as well as being enhanced by the reflected light from the snow below. This image was taken in Kuusamo in Finland, in early April.

300mm lens; ISO 100; 1/250 sec at f/8

ABOVE Cranes are very photogenic; this roosting flock of sandhill cranes was photographed at dawn through the "red mist" that can occur as the sun rises in front of steam coming off water warmer than the air temperature. This image was shot at Bosque Del Apache National Wildlife Reserve in New Mexico and won me a category at the International Wildbird Photographer of the Year competition in 2003.

500mm lens; ISO 100; 1/250 sec at f/16

the left-hand end, indicating clogged or almost clogged blacks. Don't worry about this; the aim is to achieve the shape of the bird rather than showing any plumage detail.

To achieve effective silhouettes, you ideally need to be in fairly open habitats—the flatter the better—as the best results will be shot close to sunrise or sunset. Stretches of water, deserts, estuaries, and marshes all make great locations, and waterbirds are a favorite subject for these type of images. Flocks of birds can be effective—there are really plenty of options.

Capturing Action

Action shots of birds come from knowing your subject's behavior so that you can anticipate the moments of drama. Certain times of day, particular seasons, and weather conditions can all affect behavior, so that knowledge of this, coupled with attention paid to particular birds over time, will all help.

Successful action photography has a lot to do with anticipation, and having a knowledge of bird behavior will give you this edge. The more you shoot pictures of birds, the better you will get at recognizing the signs a bird gives off before taking off—wing stretching, for example.

If the bird you are photographing is new to you, it might be that watching it for a while will reveal telltale signs of imminent behavior.

A good example of this is exhibited by the great skua: when great skuas are on their breeding grounds, they are highly territorial. When on duty at the nest, if another skua flies over, they stand, raise their wings, and call with outstretched necks. So, by sitting close to a skua's nest and watching for an approaching bird, you can ready yourself and photograph the warning display as it happens.

When fast and furious action occurs, keep your finger on the trigger. Often a fight, takeoff, or some other frenetic activity can happen so fast that the eye cannot assimilate what is going on, and it is only when you look at your pictures afterward that you realize the exact sequence of events. If the action is slow, such as a lazy wing stretch, you may have time to choose your moment and check that the

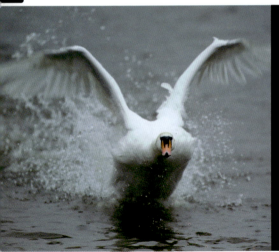

LEFT Most large birds need to take off into the wind. I moved upwind of this mute swan that showed signs of taking off.
500mm lens; ISO 320; 1/500 sec at f/8

FAR RIGHT A gray heron has just snatched a water vole. This image is not particularly esthetic, but it does illustrate a rarely witnessed piece of feeding behavior.
500mm lens; ISO 200; 1/1000 sec at f/5.6

RIGHT I noticed that each time one of these white storks got ready to depart, they would enact a bowing ritual, and the departing bird would ruffle its feathers. This was my signal to be camera-ready.
135mm lens; ISO 100; 1/1000 sec at f/8

bird is well-framed and that you have sufficient depth of field to render both the bird's body and wings sharply.

One of the temptations when you are photographing birds is to try and get too close. With action—particularly if this involves more than one bird—back off so there is plenty of space around the subject, and the picture can breathe. The other reason for backing off is to ensure that you don't cut off wing tips or have depth-of-field problems, where critical parts of a bird are out of focus. If photographing aggression or even a fight, make sure you have a fast enough shutter speed to freeze the action; most fights will need a 1/1000 sec speed to freeze movement, unless of course you want to deliberately blur the picture.

When photographing interesting behavior, it is always a trade-off between a fast enough shutter speed to cope with the movement and a small enough aperture to ensure enough depth of field. If a bird is raising its wings, yawning, or doing some other activity that is not particularly fast, if you take enough shots you might get away with a relatively slow shutter speed, thus allowing a decent depth of field.

Action photography inevitably leads to a big culling of images during the editing process. Take as many images as you can to increase your chances of capturing that one special image—believe me, when you do, it is a fantastic thrill!

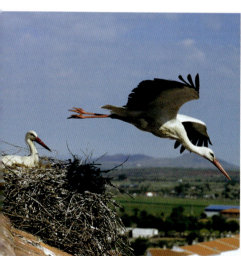

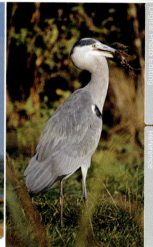

Stalking and Field Craft

For many bird photographers, stalking a bird to get a picture is a great pleasure; perhaps it is the primeval hunting instinct coming to the fore, without the desire, or the need, to actually capture the bird—except as a digital image!

Stalking is simply moving in close to a bird on foot—often by exercising stealth and the use of techniques to help communicate to the bird that you are not a threat. Successful stalking is less about pitting your wits against a bird and more about having a bird accept you into its environment, and it is immensely rewarding in itself.

Once you have spotted a bird you wish to move in close to and before you even take the first step, ensure that your camera is on, your exposure is sorted, and you are ready to take pictures. Decide, too, whether you will be kneeling or standing up, so that your tripod legs are at an appropriate height—you don't want to be in the optimum position and find you have to adjust your gear, as this may flush the bird.

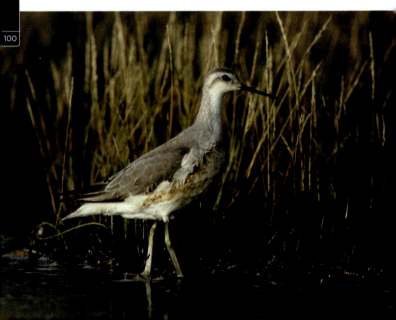

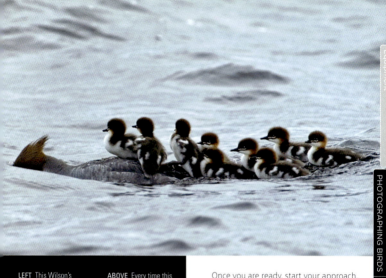

LEFT This Wilson's phalarope vagrant turned up one fall in the southwest of England. At first I found it hard to stalk, but by sitting close to its favored feeding spot, I was gradually accepted by the bird.

500mm lens; ISO 200; 1/350 sec at *f*/5.6

ABOVE Every time this female common merganser with her brood put her head underwater, searching for food, I managed to get a little closer.

500mm lens; ISO 160; 1/350 sec at *f*/6.7

Pro tip

When stalking, try not to point your lens or look directly at the bird until you are within range. If stalking a large bird, try not to shut off its escape route—remember big birds will always take off into the wind. Finally, try stalking with just your camera and tripod; don't lug your backpack with you, as this is bound to be heavy and cumbersome.

Once you are ready, start your approach, holding your tripod in front of you. Each time the bird stops feeding and looks or cranes its neck, freeze; then, once the bird is relaxed again, take a few more steps, making sure there are no sudden movements. It is a good idea not to walk directly toward your bird, but to take an angle, as the bird is likely to feel less threatened by this method. As you move closer, stop and take pictures; the bird will become used to the sound of the shutter and your presence.

With practice you will be able to detect when a bird is not comfortable and is likely to fly and, similarly, when your subject is relaxed, you will recognize the body language that reflects this. Never harass a bird that keeps flying ahead of you, because eventually it will fly away completely.

Stalking your subject often becomes a special opportunity that allows you a privileged insight into a bird's life. My first such encounter was with a snow bunting on the Isles of Scilly in England one October, which was feeding on grass seeds on some flat turf on a cliff top. At first I tried to approach, but the bird just kept flying a short distance, never allowing me to get close enough. I then decided to sit still on the edge of its favorite feeding area, and the bunting edged closer and closer, until at times it was actually too close to focus on. Clearly it perceived me as nonthreatening once I was sitting quietly, and once I was accepted, it ignored me.

Some birds favor particular spots in which to feed; for example, shorebirds often like patrolling a particular stretch of mud or sand. Near where I live there is a regular flock of sanderlings that feeds along the tide line. If I try to stalk them, they inevitably keep at an annoying distance for pictures; however, by sitting still, ahead of their feeding route along the shore, they will walk to within a few feet of me. This technique can work with a multitude of species; some, such as songbirds, may have favored perches from which they sing, so watch where they go, and then stake out your own perch and wait.

Playback of birdsong to lure songbirds has been discussed on page 85. Making sounds yourself can be equally effective. Making a "pish pish" noise repeatedly—known as "pishing"—is a common method used by birdwatchers to lure small birds into view. It works surprisingly well for some birds, particularly North American warblers. The theory is that it mimics a distressed bird mobbing a potential predator, which then draws other individuals to join in the attack.

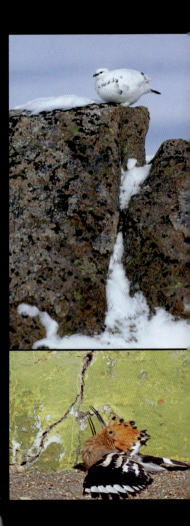

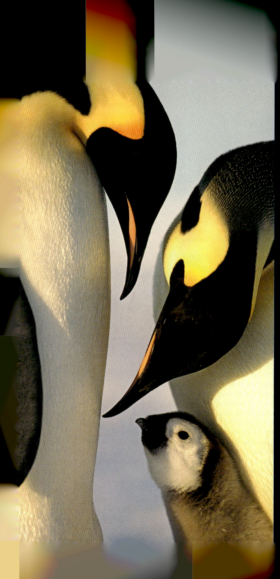

FAR LEFT Each winter I spend some time in the Scottish mountains, photographing the native wildlife there. Ptarmigan, although sometimes approachable, are often a challenge to reach when the snow is deep, but a slow, careful approach usually gets good results.

500mm lens; ISO 100; 1/500 sec at ƒ/5.6

FAR LEFT BELOW I spotted this hoopoe sunning itself against the wall of a café. By moving very cautiously a little bit at a time, taking pictures as I went, I was able to get into position and shoot a number of images.

500mm lens; ISO 100; 1/125 sec at ƒ/16

LEFT Whenever you are close to a bird that appears not to be bothered by your presence, still stay quiet and move slowly—you want your subject to be as relaxed as possible, giving you the opportunity of capturing some natural behavior. This family of emperor penguins, photographed by the Weddell Sea in Antarctica, was just a few feet away, and I still observed good field-craft by moving slowly and only when necessary.

300mm lens; ISO 50; 1/125 sec at ƒ/8

Blinds

Ranging from simple tent-like structures to more elaborate ones that can also be used as tents, blinds are the best way to get close to your subject, particularly if the bird is shy of humans. Blind "etiquette" is important, too.

Blinds have been used as a means of getting close to birds from the very start of bird photography—more than a hundred years ago, photographers were dressing up as cows and using all sorts of other disguises in their quest to get close.

We now know it is not necessary to go to such lengths of disguise. Modern blinds resemble simple tents with openings in them for pointing the lens out, and they have small viewing windows. Blinds come in various designs: some are dome-shaped and can be erected in just a couple of minutes, while others are tubular constructions that may take a bit longer to put up but are normally more rugged. There are also blinds that allow low-level work and resemble a small tent that you lie in to shoot from one end; these are good if your subject is an early riser.

Blinds used to be employed mainly for photographing birds at the nest, since nest photography was popular due to equipment limitations. Technology has improved, and nest photography is not as attractive as it once was. If you intend to place a blind for a nest, there are a few points you need to consider. It is illegal to photograph certain protected species in or near the nest without the relevant licenses. If you place your blind on private land you need permission from the landowner, and it is not usually permitted to erect blinds in most wildlife refuges and nature reserves.

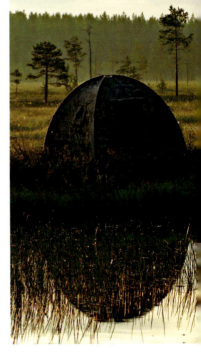

Further points to consider include moving in on the nest slowly over a number of days so the birds become acclimatized. In addition, make sure your blind is away from the public gaze—you do not want to draw attention to a nesting bird, and of course you do not want your blind stolen or vandalized.

Away from nests, blinds can be used to photograph birds that visit a particular spot on a regular basis: this may be your own backyard feeding station, a drinking pool, or perhaps a daytime roosting area. Bird photographers in America use blinds far less regularly than those in Europe. This is because so many species in America can be approached on foot without the need for

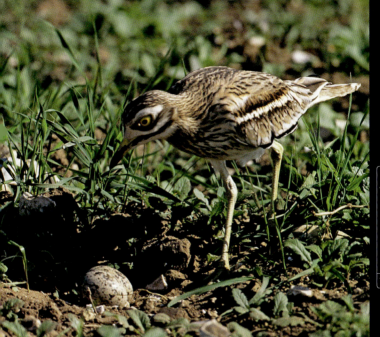

concealment, and because many good American wildlife refuges allow entry using a mobile blind in the guise of a car. In Europe the story is very different: so many birds—especially shorebirds and wildfowl—are very timid, and blind photography can often be the only option.

When positioning a blind, you need to think about the direction of the light; there is nothing more frustrating than sitting in a blind with your bird performing directly in front of you, only to find you are not quite in the right place. Think, too, about how far from the subject you want to be. Try and place the blind so that the lens you want to use will give you just the right reach. Before erecting the

ABOVE A stone curlew at her nest, photographed from a carefully placed blind. To enter the blind I asked a friend to walk me in (known as a "putter-in"), and when I wanted to leave, that person came back to accompany me out.

500mm lens; ISO 100; 1/250 sec at f/11

ABOVE LEFT A dome blind set up by a pool in Finland in order to photograph red-throated loons. An inexpensive alternative to a dedicated blind is army camouflage netting. Although harder to set up and requiring more experience in terms of knowing where to place it, camouflage can be very effective and is readily available through army surplus stores.

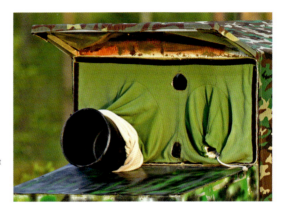

RIGHT It is a good idea, when leaving a blind unattended, to leave a "dummy" lens, such as a bit of pipe, sticking out from one of the apertures. This ensures the birds get used to a protrusion.

blind, set up your lens and experiment with distances. Find as flat a piece of ground as possible, since you don't want to be tipping in your chair, and when choosing a chair go for one with a backrest rather than using an uncomfortable stool. I always pick chairs with decent-sized feet, too, as you do not want one half of the chair sinking into soft ground.

The blind may need some extra concealment for some species; bracken or tree branches can be laid across to help break up its outline. Place a dummy lens sticking out when the blind is not in use, so the birds get used to a protrusion—this can be an old bit of plastic pipe or something similar. Depending on your subject, you may need a friend to see you in and then leave once installed. This is because most birds cannot count, so when your friend walks away, they will think the coast is clear. Once in the blind, do not stick your lens out too far, and avoid making sudden movements; this is particularly important with very wary species, such as birds of prey. If using a blind in winter, wrap up warm and, most importantly, wear warm footwear—feet can become very cold when

Pro tip

Comfort in a blind is paramount, since you are likely to be spending a few hours at a time sitting still. I have mentioned the need for a decent seat, but ensure too that you are well wrapped up for winter sessions. Feeling cold, and especially having cold feet or a cold head, can make a session in a blind a feat of endurance, which is not conducive to concentrating on photography.

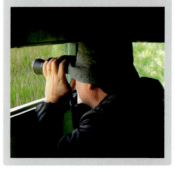

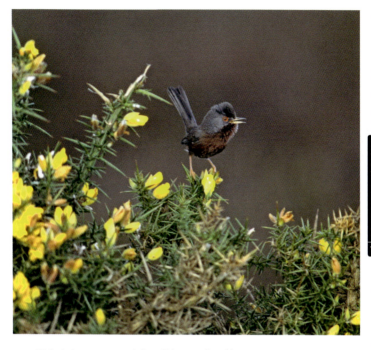

ABOVE This Dartford warbler sang regularly from the same perch on a gorse bush, so I placed a blind close by and simply waited for the bird to arrive and perform. I have included a reasonable amount of the bush in the frame, as the yellow flowers add color to the image.

500mm lens; ISO 100; 1/500 sec at f/5.6

you are sitting still for a number of hours. Finally, don't forget a urine bottle if you need to be in the blind all day.

Many reserves have public blinds; some can be great for bird photography, while others can be awful. Talk to other photographers to seek out the good ones; most reserves have at least one blind that will prove fruitful.

Cars make great mobile blinds—many birds fail to associate danger with a vehicle, and the great thing about a car is that you can cover a lot of ground. I use a beanbag balanced on the door frame as support for my long lens, and you can buy window mounts (see page 38). Some photographers even manage to set their tripods up in the passenger seat, although I have never worked out how to do this satisfactorily.

Unlike stalking on foot, when it is best to move in close in stages, once you have spotted a bird from the car it is better to go for broke and freewheel up to the bird with the engine off, at the optimum distance for a shot. The intermittent engine noise caused by stopping and starting can increase your subject's anxiety otherwise, causing it to fly away. Before you move in on the bird, be prepared with your equipment. Make sure you have the right lens on, that your exposure is sorted, and that you are ready to shoot—leaving all this until you are in position is a recipe for failure.

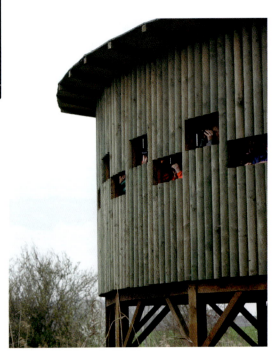

LEFT Large public blinds, found in many wildlife reserves, can get very busy, making it difficult to photograph. However, you shouldn't dismiss them out of hand. If you're new to bird photography they can be a good way to improve your craft.

RIGHT I used my car as a blind to photograph this black woodpecker's nest. The tree was conveniently situated right next to a forest track.

500mm lens; ISO 100; 1/125 sec at f/5.6

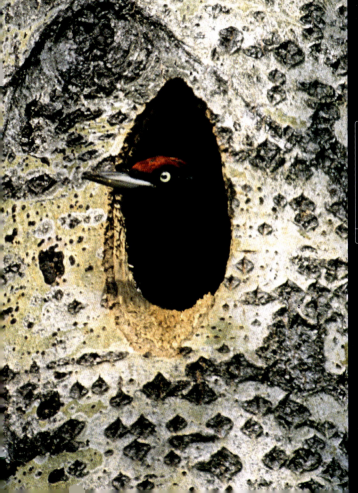

Remote-control Photography

Triggering the camera with a remote control gives you another option for getting in close to your subject. Some preparation in setting up the system is involved, but a static camera fitted with a wide-angle lens can pay dividends.

The big advantage of using a remote-control rig, as opposed to a blind, is the ability to use a wide-angle lens and capture the bird within its habitat. Plenty of planning and fine-tuning is usually necessary to successfully take such shots, and the main requirement is a bird or birds that visit the same perch or spot regularly.

A lot of my remote-control work is done at my feeding stations, where I photograph garden birds in garden settings and on feeders; the advantage in this setting is that I can entice a bird to an exact spot or onto the feeder I want. I normally stand a little way back—or sit in a blind close by, my preferred method. Because my garden birds are continually visiting and tolerate plenty of disturbance, I can check the picture compositions on the camera's LCD regularly, until I have the desired result.

With shier species it is best to take as many images as possible. This is because, unlike viewing a bird through the viewfinder of your camera, with a remote-control setup it is difficult to judge your ideal moment for taking an image, thus your failure rate will inevitably be higher.

I fire the trigger with a wireless transmitter, which works to a range of more than 400 feet; this allows me to be a long way back if necessary. You do not have to go to the expense of a wireless outfit. Infrared triggers

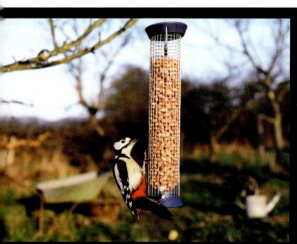

LEFT Remote-control photography only works reliably when you can be sure exactly where your bird will perch, as here with this great spotted woodpecker on a feeder.

90mm lens; ISO 50; 1/60 sec at *f*/11

can be purchased, but these do need a good line of sight and can struggle to work well in very bright conditions. You can buy very cheap triggers that extend for fifteen feet or so and are operated by squeezing a rubber bulb that forces air to push the trigger. These screw into your camera's shutter button or onto the body. They can be a little unreliable, and you need to be in a blind very close by, but they are worth considering if you want to experiment with the technique.

Your camera needs to be set up on a tripod or use other support; I often place mine on a beanbag if taking ground-level shots. Remote photography's wide angles mean the camera has to be placed very close to where your bird will perch. This means your subject may end up being rather suspicious of the camera initially, and may not readily use the

perch. If so, you either need to use a dummy camera and lens and move it into position over a number of days or use a soundproofed box, known as a "blimp." This can be a box made of plywood that fits over your camera and is lined with polystyrene or foam. The advantage of a blimp is that it softens the sound of the shutter and will protect the camera from the elements.

Once the camera is in position, I use the depth-of-field preview button on my camera to accurately set the focus, for both the subject and background. Metering can sometimes be tricky, so I tend to set the camera on autoexposure.

There is a high failure rate with this type of photography, but it only takes one image for the effort to be worthwhile. The technique certainly produces pictures with a difference.

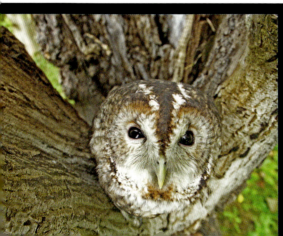

LEFT To take this unusual view of a roosting tawny owl in a hollowed-out tree, I placed a remote-controlled camera with 35mm lens above the spot where this owl regularly roosted during the night, when the owl was out hunting. I then returned during the day and triggered the camera to bag my shot. The sound of the shutter made the owl look up at the camera, which was an added bonus.

35mm lens; ISO 160; 1/125 sec at ƒ/2.8; triggered by Pocket Wizard wireless transmitter

Traveling with your Gear by Air

Bird photography brings a whole new aspect to traveling abroad, with chances to see and capture new and exciting species. Transporting your precious equipment is an anxiety, but with a little forethought and preparation, most worries are needless.

Few of us find it relaxing to travel through airports with heavy photo backpacks. There is always the lingering danger of an overzealous official banishing our precious gear to the aircraft hold—and once in an aircraft hold, photo gear is in the lap of the gods and any number of worrying fates may await.

Unless you are using a specially strengthened case such as a Pelicase, it is imperative not to let your gear be taken from you at check-in. There are all sorts of ploys you can use to avoid this, but it is a good start to use a backpack designed to fit the maximum dimensions dictated by the airlines. I currently use a Lowepro Nature Trekker that fits these requirements perfectly and is just shallow enough to fit under a seat on most aircraft, which is very useful if you fail to find space in the overhead bins.

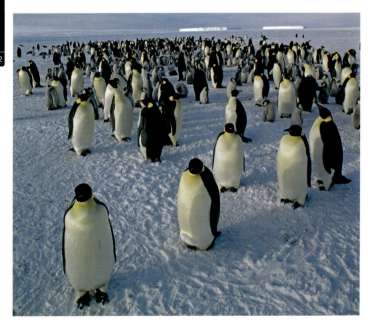

Pro tip

When traveling on airlines, especially in the United States where passengers carry on items far larger than those in Europe, try to be one of the first on the plane so there is space to stow your bag in the overhead bins. When bin space runs out, late-arriving passengers regularly have their carry-on luggage taken off them and stowed in the hold—a conflict you want to avoid. Here my camera bag is being attacked by some juvenile delinquents—striated caracaras or johnny rooks as they are known on the Falklands, where this was taken. I never take with me more than I can comfortably carry for at least half a day.

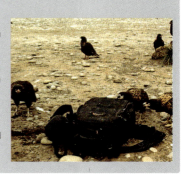

At check-in, you are often asked to identify your carry-on luggage; I always try and make this look as light as possible! If it does get weighed, it is inevitably well over the limit—this is always the crucial point, but I have yet to have my bag removed from me. I simply explain politely that the bag contains hugely valuable and delicate camera gear; this is normally enough, but if still challenged I point out that the gear is not insured when in an aircraft hold under my insurance policy, and so will the airline agree to cover costs if it is lost or damaged? This last line of defence always works for me; however, if one day it does not, I will be ready, wearing my jacket with lots of big pockets so I can off-load as much as possible before the bag hits the weight limit.

LEFT The stresses of traveling to far-flung destinations on once-in-a-lifetime bird photography trips are soon forgotten when you are confronted with great photo opportunities, such as this emperor penguin colony on the Weddell Sea in Antarctica.

24mm lens: ISO 100; 1/250 sec at f/11

Some photographers use photo vests when they are traveling and cram as much as they can into these. I have a friend who wraps his long lens up in bubble wrap and carries it in a duty-free bag, along with his regular camera bag. I can always fit all the gear I will need from day to day in my backpack, but can never fit a spare camera body, chargers, and other paraphernalia needed. I often carefully pack these items in my hard-cased suitcase, which gives adequate protection.

Obviously, insure all your equipment to make sure that anything damaged while on your trip will be replaced free of charge. In case of theft, make a note of the serial numbers, makes, and models, and consider taking digital photos of your equipment to help with identification. In the United States, registering your equipment with your local customs office is recommended. This provides you with proof of ownership and removes the possibility of having to pay import duty on your gear when you return, if customs wrongly assume you've purchased it abroad.

Choosing Bird Photography Vacations

Setting off on your own to find and photograph birds in a foreign country can be rather daunting; specialized bird-photography vacations are designed to take away the everyday stresses, allowing you to concentrate on taking the pictures.

Years ago I would listen in awe to tales from pioneering bird photographers of expeditions to southern Spain, Lapland, and other exotic-sounding destinations. Today, such locations can be visited cheaply on budget airlines for a weekend! Not only has the ease of travel changed, but so has the flow of information on where to go to take pictures. The Internet is a big source of information for finding out about these opportunities, as is talking to other photographers.

When looking at vacations for bird photography, the very best are those that are run specifically for photographers. There are plenty of birdwatching vacations that suggest good photographic opportunities, but these trips are set up primarily for watching birds, not photographing them. It will soon become frustrating as most of the group will want to move on to see the next bird, not giving you the opportunity to make the most of the photographic potential. If you are a sharp digiscoper then these trips are ideal, as you don't need to wait until everyone has finished watching the bird before you move closer.

Since nothing in bird photography is guaranteed, you cannot always expect success, but a lot of hard work has normally gone into setting up bird-photography vacations: food being put out daily, blinds constructed, and so on. It should come as no surprise, then, to learn that many such trips are expensive. Joining a group with a leader may be the only cost-effective option for some destinations such as Peru, Japan, or the Antarctic. This brings many benefits: the cost

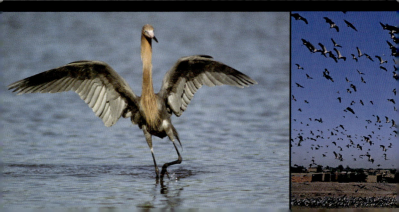

is brought down from that of independent travel (or at least it should be); you have a leader who can assist with your photography, and the opportunities should be set up so that you don't need to find the birds or figure out other logistical problems on your own.

When choosing a trip, check that your leader knows the destination well. Also try to chat with photographers who have been before, or to the leader to get a feel of how the trip will be run—if you are spending a lot, you want to make sure opportunities will be maximized. The best companies are those that pay their leaders well; some refrain from paying, stating that a free trip is payment enough. I would think twice about investing in these, as your leader may be more focused on taking his own pictures than helping clients. Finally, it is easy to visit many destinations on your own or with like-minded friends, such as Florida or Lesbos in the Greek Islands.

FAR LEFT This reddish egret photo was taken in Florida, one of the world's top destinations for bird photography. The Sunshine State is an easy destination to visit and photograph by yourself or with a group of friends, and the birds pose few problems, since they are incredibly tame.

500mm lens; ISO 100; 1/1000 sec at *f*/8

CENTRE Foreign travel can introduce you to some of the world's great bird spectacles. These are demoiselle cranes that come to eat grain put out for them by the villagers of Khichan in India during the winter.

24mm lens; ISO 200; 1/500 sec at *f*/11

BELOW These king penguins were at St. Andrews Bay on the remote island of South Georgia. When booking such a trip, find out as much as you can about the flexibility of the group and, particularly on cruises, how much time you will get ashore, as this can vary from a whole day to just an hour or two.

17–35mm zoom; ISO 100; 1/250 sec at *f*/11

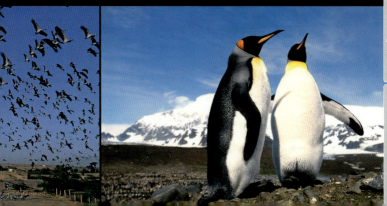

Digiscoping Techniques in the Field

The results obtainable from a compact digital camera linked to a telescope can be terrific and not possible on even an expensive DSLR. Although The system brings about its own ways of working, these techniques still take their cue from standard good practice.

Due to the limitations of following fast-moving birds in the viewfinder with a digiscope, photographing active subjects, such as warblers and other small birds, can take a lot of practice. Even so, all birds stop and rest occasionally to preen or look around, so you need to stay alert and be patient. If you are new to digiscoping, it is worth starting with shorebirds or larger, less-active species.

Set the various parameters on your compact camera before you start shooting; these include sharpening levels, the white balance, the ISO, and selecting the appropriate JPEG quality. Most point-and-shoot compacts perform poorly at high ISO settings compared with DSLRs, due to their small chips and inferior processing algorithms; this means that noise can be a problem above ISO 200. It is advisable to switch off the ISO auto setting and leave it on its lowest setting, probably 100.

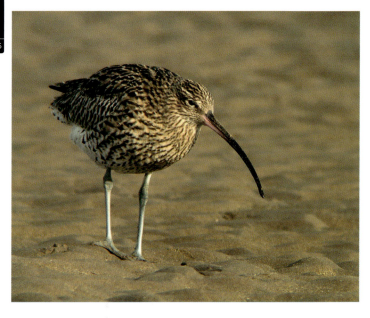

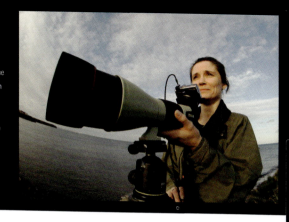

Like DSLR users, most digiscopers set their white balance to auto, and this works well 99 percent of the time. Setting your metering is a personal preference, but spot-metering on the autofocus area is common among digiscopers. I would suggest leaving your image sharpening on "normal," as you can always sharpen in Photoshop if necessary. Image quality should be set at the finest, least-compressed setting, normally referred to as "fine."

As mentioned previously, there is no substitute for a good, sturdy tripod. This is absolutely essential for digiscopers, since the high magnifications you will be shooting at magnify any shake, creating blurry pictures. If camera shake is a problem, try kneeling with the tripod legs folded to their lowest working height, particularly if it is very windy. When using very slow shutter speeds, a cable release will help—if you have a rock-solid tripod and no wind when using a cable release, shutter speeds as low as 1/15 sec should achieve sharp results, as long as your bird is not moving. If you don't have a shutter-release cable, try the self-timer, although this method has to be used in the hope that the bird is aware it is not allowed to move! The decision-making processes for choosing shutter speed and aperture should be the same as for conventional photography.

As with conventional photography, the autofocus on your camera may sometimes hunt if it cannot find enough contrast, so be aware of this and move your focusing point on the bird if this creates a problem. The camera's focus confirmation will help in sharp focusing.

In bright conditions, monitor shades can be invaluable. Nikon makes a handy little shade that slips over the Coolpix monitor, which you can keep in a pocket or attached to the camera so it is always handy.

Heat haze can be a big problem when you are some distance from the bird. On hot days, try to avoid shooting across tarmac or other substrates that soak up and so give off lots of heat. Of course, heat haze is difficult to combat during the middle of the day, so shooting early or later on can help.

In the Field—A Personal Experience

When you start photographing birds, you may have a clear idea of what you want to shoot and how you want to shoot it. However, by regularly reviewing your goals and keeping an eye out for unexpected opportunities, you give your craft every chance to improve in ways that you might not have anticipated.

For many years, my constant aim when I set off on bird photography trips was to shoot as many different species as I could. This worked well for me and gave me a great deal of satisfaction. However, in the back of my mind I often had a lurking feeling that many of my shots might have been compromised in my quest for variety.

This approach fundamentally changed when, in spring 1988, I attempted to photograph a drake king eider on the Ythan Estuary, north of Aberdeen in Scotland. I spent two whole days taking images of this bird, but there was one particular shot I wanted: the bird's colorful head poking above a breaking wave in the foreground. After much persistence I finally got my shot, and I realized from that day on that if I had a vision of an image, it was possible to go out and work at it until I captured it.

Ten years later saw me joining an expedition to the Weddell Sea in Antarctica to photograph emperor penguins. This trip lasted almost a month and was an endurance test on mind, body, and equipment. For ten days I was totally immersed in photographing the penguins, and I came away with a body of work that won a number of awards. To this day, these images remain some of my finest pieces. This too was a watershed in the way that I worked, and since then I have put all my energies into acquiring as deep a coverage of a species as I can.

I have found that by putting time and effort into being in the field, great opportunities present themselves, and image concepts can be worked at and achieved. A more recent image that illustrates this is that of the flying dipper to the right.

Dippers fly very fast, so they are hard to capture in flight using conventional techniques. I decided to photograph dippers along a stretch of river in Derbyshire, England,

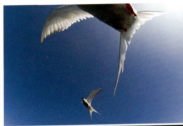

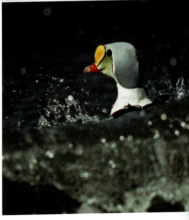

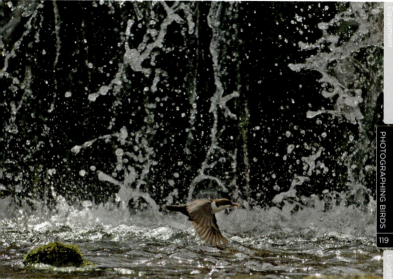

ABOVE This white-throated dipper image came from three days of persevering in front of the waterfall.

70–200mm zoom; ISO 400; 1/2000 sec at ƒ/4

LEFT This image of a king eider fighting through the waves, taken almost two decades ago, changed my entire approach to photographing birds. I realized that with perseverance I could achieve the images I had preplanned in my imagination.

600mm lens; ISO 100; 1/250 sec at ƒ/5.6

ABOVE LEFT My photographic aim is always to try to design an image, rather than aimlessly snapping away at my subjects. I purposely included just part of the closest arctic tern in this image—less is often more.

10.5mm lens; ISO 200; 1/800 sec at ƒ/11

one spring, and spent a number of days on the riverbank working with the birds. I wanted to illustrate the dipper within its habitat, and one afternoon when I noticed a dipper fly across the face of the waterfall, I knew then that this was the shot I wanted. I then stood for around eight hours every day for the next three days, firing off shots as the occasional bird flew in front of the falls. Most opportunities ended with the bird flying at the wrong height or veering off-course at the last moment. Eventually, however, everything came together and I bagged my shot; my doggedness to get the shot had worked.

For me, one of the great thrills of shooting in the field is not knowing what opportunity will come next. I expect the unexpected, and just hope to be ready for it.

DIGITAL PHOTO EDITING

Welcome to the digital darkroom! This section of the book shows you what to do with your images once they enter the computer—how to improve the way they look, tricks of the trade for improving composition, and how to become an eye doctor, too.

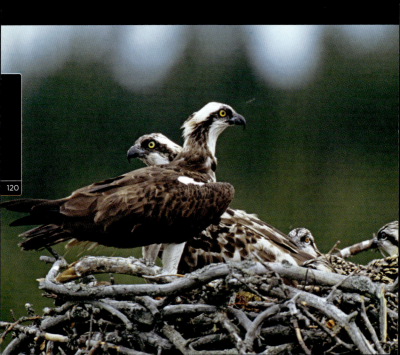

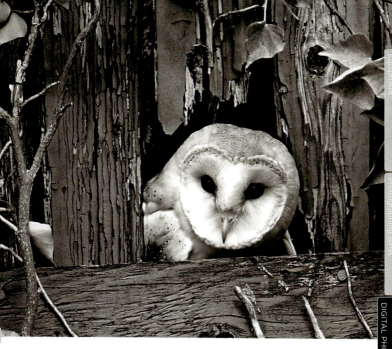

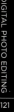

In the mid-1980s, bird magazines were still predominantly printed in black and white, and so I and many of my peers were shooting in this medium as well as in color. I started out using black-and-white film and had to learn the ways of the traditional darkroom. Photography is now dominated by color and computers, but still we have a darkroom to work in—in the form of computer imaging software. As in the days of black and white, learning how to optimize our images is just as important as learning how to take them in the first place.

One of the reasons that many bird photographers stuck to using film for so long when the advantages of digital were obvious, was undoubtedly the apprehension of the unknown. If computers are new to you, digital imaging can offer a steep learning curve. This challenge is less daunting, however, when you realize many of the processes are all about using common sense and judgment as to what you think looks right on the screen.

As mentioned in the introduction, all the processes follow the latest version of Adobe Photoshop. However, if you are a Photoshop Elements user or use other software, both the tools and processes are either similar or in many cases identical, so you should have no problem following the directions.

OPPOSITE A pair of ospreys in the nest, with several young.

ABOVE A monochrome image of a barn owl.

Computer Hardware

As if the advances in digital cameras aren't enough to contend with, computers and software seem to be upgraded every week. To navigate this technological jungle, it pays to be clear on the few basic requirements that will enable you to store and manipulate your images.

If you have a computer or are intending to buy one, you need to be sure it will be up to the task of dealing with your pictures. This means having plenty of RAM (random access memory) and a decent processing speed.

RAM is used to run the programs in your computer and is where your images go when being viewed and manipulated; in effect, it is a temporary storage area within your computer. RAM is easy to add to a computer if you already have an existing machine; if not, make sure your new computer ends up with at least 2Gb (gigabyte) of memory—you should

really load on as much as you can afford. For Photoshop to operate at a minimum level, for example, it requires five times more RAM than the size of the file you're working on. An image file of around 13Mb (a typical Raw file from a 12 megapixel camera) would require a minimum 65Mb of available RAM, bearing in mind that some RAM will be taken up by the operating system and any other programs that are open simultaneously. CS5 requires a minimum of 1Gb of RAM.

In terms of processing speed, in a broad sense the more gigahertz (GHz) your computer has, the faster it will be able to process data. However, many modern processors employ a number of "cores." Each core is a separate processor chip, so a computer with two cores can—theoretically—do twice as much in the same time.

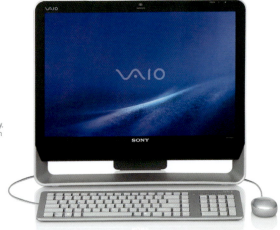

RIGHT There is a huge choice of computer hardware available today, and it is wise to research any potential purchase carefully before buying.

Scanners

Many of you may have images that exist only as film (either negatives or transparencies). Film requires scanning to convert the analog information (the film) into digital data. This can be done either by using an external lab or using your own scanner. If relying on an external lab, use one that has a drum scanner, as this will provide the best possible quality. If you want to purchase your own scanner, the choice is between a flatbed or film scanner. As their name suggests, flatbed scanners are designed primarily for scanning flat media, such as paper or prints. This doesn't exclude them from scanning film (with the use of an adapter), but it makes them less than ideal. If you have a good deal of film to scan, a dedicated film scanner is the route to go. These are designed specifically for scanning transparencies and negatives. The best quality will come from a virtual drum scanner, but these may be prohibitively expensive. Always make sure that the film is clean of dust and dirt prior to scanning. Scan in Adobe RGB or LAB color modes and at the highest possible resolution. Save the file in TIFF or native Photoshop (.psd) format, never in JPEG.

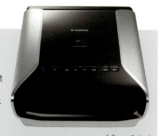

A Canon flatbed scanner.

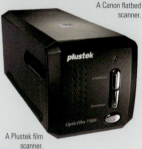

A Plustek film scanner.

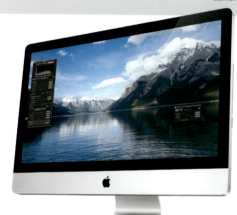

LEFT Historically, professionals working in design-led fields, including photographers, have used Apple Macintosh computers. However, today there's little to choose between an Apple Macintosh computer and a Windows PC.

The next issue to examine is hard drive space: a minimum of 500Gb with an 8Mb (megabyte) disk cache gives both speed and good capacity. If you take lots of pictures, your hard disk will soon be groaning under the strain, so, as with RAM, more is better. Whether you go for a Windows or Apple Macintosh system is a personal preference. Adobe Photoshop or Photoshop Elements, the imaging software you are likely to use, works equally well on either system.

If you are really serious about your photography, an important consideration is the quality of the monitor you use to view and enhance your images. LCD (liquid crystal display) technology has advanced sufficiently in recent times that they are now generally preferred over the bulkier CRT (cathode-ray tube) type; the former flat-screen type is without flicker, has less glare, and takes up less space. Whichever screen you decide to go for, you should try for a minimum screen size of 17 or 19 inches. The bigger the better here, and not just physically, but in terms of pixels too; a 19-inch screen with 800 x 600 pixels is not as good as a 19-inch screen with 1280 x 1024 pixels. Another important consideration is the number of colors the monitor is capable of displaying (it should be in the millions).

Finally, a word on laptops: they are very popular with traveling photographers, and the latest models from Sony and Apple have excellent screens, too. One thing to remember when viewing images on laptops is their narrow angle of view.

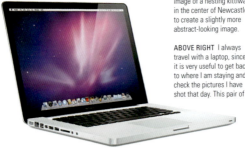

BELOW RIGHT Your computer opens the door to a new way of making eye-catching images. I have played around with the colors and contrast in this image of a nesting kittiwake in the center of Newcastle to create a slightly more abstract-looking image.

ABOVE RIGHT I always travel with a laptop, since it is very useful to get back to where I am staying and check the pictures I have shot that day. This pair of

great blue herons was taken at the Venice Rookery in Florida. The bird stretching its wings is a fledgling.

600mm lens; ISO 100; 1/800 sec at f/5.6

ABOVE AND LEFT Most professional and many keen amateur photographers now carry around a laptop with them when photographing away from home. Small and portable, you can use them to store images, undertake editing work, and even upload pictures to websites or other hosting sites.

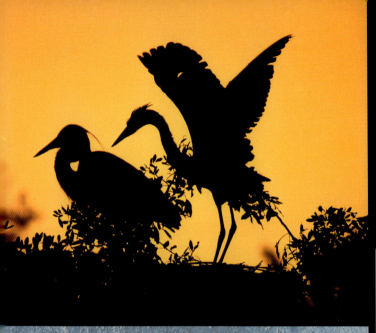

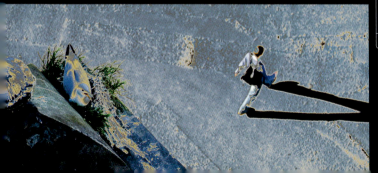

Editing Software and Working with Color

There are numerous editing programs on the market, but Adobe's Photoshop has been and still is the market leader, and for good reason. Remember that no matter how good your editing suite, if the colors on your monitor are not accurate, your results will be disappointing.

Once you have transferred your images from camera to computer, you need a way of organizing, editing, and optimizing, before finally storing them for future use. Adobe Photoshop is the top choice—indeed there are no rivals for what it offers. At first glance it is a daunting program, yet you only need to learn a few simple Photoshop procedures to effectively enhance your images. You will find that as your experience with the program develops, you delve deeper and discover new, exciting tools to develop your creativity.

There is a basic and inexpensive version of Photoshop, called Photoshop Elements, that will do all you need for basic image adjustments. However, if you can afford it, go for the full, professional version—at the time of writing this is CS5. This will allow you to develop your skills as you progress, and when new versions of Photoshop are released with developments that may be useful, then you can upgrade easily.

BELOW Photoshop Elements is an affordable, "cut-down" version of Photoshop. Despite lacking some of the features of the full version, Photoshop Elements, which is available for both Mac and PCs is a very capable image-editing suite.

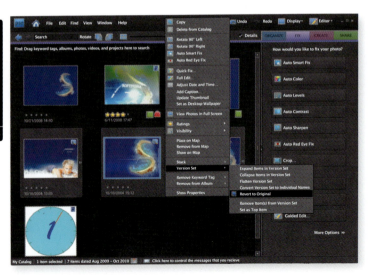

Raw workflow software

More and more photographers, both professionals and amateurs alike, are turning to workflow-based software such as Adobe's Lightroom and Apple's Aperture. Both programs are more than just image editing software, they are designed to be a "one-stop" photographer's shop. You import your images (both programs will convert Raw files), review them, make any adjustments you want, including localized adjustments to tone and color, and prepare them for output for either web or print. Both programs also feature image-management areas that allow you to batch name, categorize, add tags, and so on, enabling you to easily organize your photographs however you want.

New features in the latest versions include watermarking, non-destructive perspective and lens correction, tethered shooting (ideal for studio work), and new, more flexible printing options.

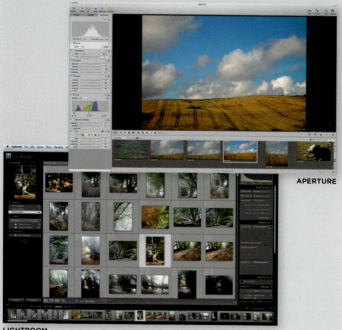

APERTURE

LIGHTROOM

The alternatives to using Photoshop are camera manufacturers' software: Canon and Nikon both produce their own, and Apple offers Aperture, which is designed for use on Apple Macintosh computers and aimed at professional photographers. It is focused on the Raw work flow and offers an all-in-one post-production tool. Adobe's Lightroom also manages Raw workflow and is well worth considering. Aperture and Lightroom will, for many photographers, offer an alternative to using the full version of Photoshop, as these new tools are designed specifically with photographers in mind.

To get good, consistent results, whether printing your images or sending them to others to view, you need to be able to trust the colors you see on your screen; this is color management. Color is a subjective thing, and if you regularly watch birds you will know how lighting during different times in the day affects the colors of the birds we view, so you may be forgiven for wondering whether color management actually matters to you. But do you want to produce prints that consistently replicate what is displayed on your screen? Do you want to display on your screen the colors that you saw on the bird you photographed accurately? If the answer to these two questions is yes, you need to color-manage both your monitor and printer.

Using the display calibrator is a big step in the right direction for calibrating a Mac monitor. If you are a Windows user, Adobe Gamma, which ships with Windows versions of Photoshop, will do the same job. This software is found in Preferences > Control Panel and adjusts the brightness, black, white, midpoints, color temperature, and sets the gamma. If you do nothing else, this will help.

To be really accurate with color, you need to use a colorimeter or spectrophotometer. These are devices that attach to your monitor's screen and read colored targets, generating a color profile known as an International Color Consortium profile (ICC). Having these profiles as standards means all devices color-calibrated in this way can speak the same color language. This means that if you send a picture to a friend's computer, and both of your monitors are color-calibrated, the image should appear as a very close match.

Consider your work setup too. Avoid direct sunlight spilling across your screen or very changeable light conditions within the room. Subdued lighting is best for accurately gauging the adjustments you make to your images; I use a hood on my screen to cut down on reflections.

Finally, you should ensure that if you are capturing your images in the Adobe RGB (1998) color space; this same color space should be set to Photoshop or whichever software you decide to use.

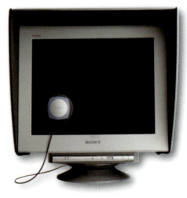

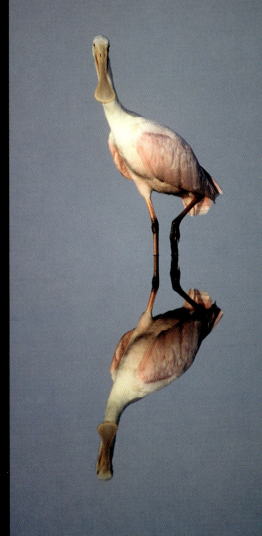

RIGHT Color accuracy is important: the subtle pinks of this roseate spoonbill could look very different from reality on a monitor that is not calibrated.

500mm lens; ISO 100; 1/250 sec at f/11

LEFT Calibration devices fit onto the screen and match the screen representation to Pantone-correct colors. This is a specialized Sony calibration monitor, where the device comes ready-fitted.

Importing, Sorting, and Editing

Every photographer who uses digital media has, at one time or another, lost images on a memory card or deleted image files on a computer. Once done, the pain of the loss means you make sure it doesn't happen again, but it's better to lower the odds of it happening in the first place.

Once back home from a shooting trip, you need to download your valuable images to a computer as soon as you can. There are various methods of doing this; perhaps the most obvious way, but one to avoid is downloading directly from camera to computer via a USB port. This is a very slow method, and I would really only suggest it as a last resort.

It is better to use a PC card adapter, which allows your memory cards to be inserted into a PC card slot on a laptop or PC card reader, or you can use an external card reader. I use a universal card reader plugged into my computer, into which my CompactFlash card is inserted for a swift download of images.

Once your images are safely on your computer, you can ready your card for reuse by formatting it. This wipes it clean. If you happen to do this by mistake and lose images, there is retrieval software available. Lexar CompactFlash cards contain Image Rescue software, and some other brands ship with a CD that can be used for retrieval. Alternatively, there are many websites on the Internet offering solutions.

Once you have downloaded your images into a folder, you need to take a critical look at them to do an initial edit and discard any obvious howlers. Because I use Photoshop, I use Bridge. This is Photoshop's file browser, and it offers a powerful means of reviewing images. This and many other software programs provide a slide-show facility, and this is my preferred way of editing quickly. By passing the images through the slide show, those that are unsharp or inadequate in other ways can be deleted, until you finally end up with a selection to be processed and eventually archived.

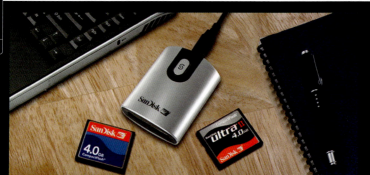

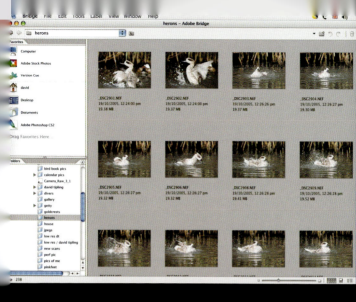

LEFT Using a card reader, such as this one from SanDisk, makes transferring images from your memory cards to your computer much quicker, and is more convenient than plugging in your camera.

ABOVE I use Bridge, Photoshop's file browser, to make an initial trawl through my images once they have downloaded.

RIGHT The slide show is an ideal way of assessing your images with a view to making an initial edit.

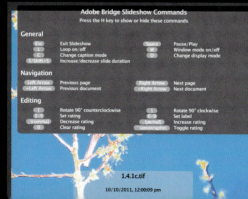

Adobe Bridge Slideshow Commands
Press the H key to show or hide these commands

General

ESC	Exit Slideshow
L	Loop on/off
C	Change caption mode
S/Shift+S	Increase/decrease slide duration

Space	Pause/Play
W	Window mode on/off
D	Change display mode

Navigation

Left Arrow	Previous page
←Left Arrow	Previous document

Right Arrow	Next page
→Right Arrow	Next document

Editing

[	Rotate 90° counterclockwise
1–5	Set rating
, (comma)	Decrease rating
0	Clear rating

]	Rotate 90° clockwise
6–9	Set label
. (period)	Increase rating
' (apostrophe)	Toggle rating

1.4.1c.tif

10/10/2011, 12:00:09 pm

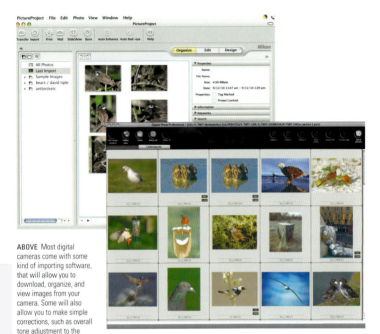

ABOVE Most digital cameras come with some kind of importing software, that will allow you to download, organize, and view images from your camera. Some will also allow you to make simple corrections, such as overall tone adjustment to the images, but for a more advanced and detailed level of correction you will need some dedicated image-editing software.

Do not get too ruthless in your editing, because it often pays to revisit images at a later date to take another look. It is surprising how your attitude can change toward an image over the passage of time. I sometimes look back at images taken years ago, which at the time I was not keen on, and suddenly see them in a different light. Perhaps this is often because a fresh memory of looking at a bird through the viewfinder doesn't compare well with then viewing it on screen. I never cull images that are technically perfect or reasonably composed, since although I might not choose to process them, I may have a use for them in the future.

Pro tip

Once you have completed your edit, it will help to get into the habit of renumbering your images to follow whichever system you use. You do not want to end up with images on your hard drive with the same sequence number. This will happen unless you renumber, because DSLRs reset themselves once they reach a limit, normally 9,999. When renumbering, limit yourself to a total of eight characters whether numeric or alphabetic in total. This is because some environments do not support file names in excess of eight characters, so you might send someone an image with more than eight characters in the file name and find it cannot be read by their computer.

Once you've made your initial selection, it's time to start processing your images. As discussed earlier, you'll need a dedicated image-editing program to prepare your images for final output, whether to print or for the web. Most programs are available to download free for trial periods so you can see if it's the right editor for you.

Alternatively, you could see if the software bundled with your computer does the trick. For example, Macs will have a version of iPhoto, which can perform basic tasks such as cropping, while PCs often come loaded with Picasa from Google, which provides a similar level of adjustment. There are also a good number of free image-editors for both Mac and PC. A quick search on the Internet will soon provide you with a list.

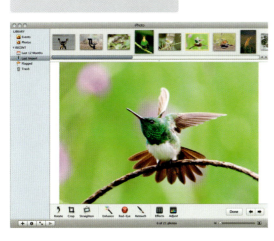

LEFT iPhoto is part of the iLife package, which comes bundled with new Apple Mac computers. Although not as sophisticated as programs such as Photoshop Elements, PaintShop Pro or Photoshop, it may possibly be all you need.

Processing a Raw Image

With all its different controls, Photoshop can appear daunting at the start, but each command has a specific task. Once you learn these tasks, it becomes second nature to follow certain paths in Photoshop to process the image from your DSLR.

If your camera allows you to shoot in Raw, then I would strongly urge you to do so. While it is more time-consuming to deal with a Raw image, you do have far greater control over the final result.

To open a Raw image you need a Raw converter. This is built into Photoshop for most makes of camera, and is called Adobe Camera Raw (ACR). A few require a software plug-in that can be downloaded for free from the Adobe website. While I use Adobe Camera Raw, you will hear other photographers championing other third party converters; such as Breeze Browser, Capture One, and

Bibble to name just three. However, I have no complaints with ACR, and when used in conjunction with Photoshop's file browser, Bridge, it is well suited to my workflow.

ACR is illustrated here (with the top Toolbar and lower file information line blown up), but other Raw converters will have similar if not identical tools, so my suggestions are applicable to these too. The file information line shows your color space, usually Adobe

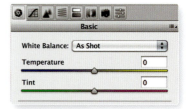

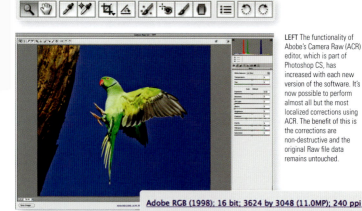

LEFT The functionality of Abobe's Camera Raw (ACR) editor, which is part of Photoshop CS, has increased with each new version of the software. It's now possible to perform almost all but the most localized corrections using ACR. The benefit of this is the corrections are non-destructive and the original Raw file data remains untouched.

Adobe RGB (1998); 16 bit; 3624 by 3048 (11.0MP); 240 ppi

RGB (1998); bit depth (preserving 16-bits per channel); the size of the file (here 3624 x 3048 pixels—11MP); and the resolution, here 240ppi. Clicking on the line will bring up the Raw Workflow Options, where you can select alternative Color Spaces, bit-depth, file sizes, and resolution should you wish.

A number of tools run along the top left of the screen. On the left, the *Magnify* tool will, when double-clicked, enlarge the image to 100 percent, while next door, the *Hand*, when double-clicked, will restore the image—this tool can be used to scroll around an enlarged image on-screen. Other useful tools include a *Crop* tool, a *Straighten* tool, a *Spot Removal* tool, a *Red Eye Removal* tool, the *Adjustment Brush*, for making localized adjustments, and a *Graduated Filter* tool, which works in a similar way to the *Adjustment Brush*, but is applied in a different way. Finally there is the *Preferences* box, to bring up the Raw preferences dialog window, and tools to rotate the image.

A useful view option is *Preview*, which allows you to see adjustments you are making to the image as you do them, while another option is the *Full Screen Mode* button, which allows you to toggle between from full to reduced screen mode.

The real power of ACR is found down the right side, under a series of eight tabs, under each of which are found a variety of controls. The most useful settings are found under the Basic tab.

When you open a Raw image in ACR you will notice that, with the exception of *White Balance* and *Saturation*, the four main settings (*Exposure*, *Shadows*, *Brightness*, and *Contrast*) are all preadjusted automatically by Camera Raw. This is the software's best guess at how the image should look and, in many cases, is a pretty good starting point. However, as with most things automatic, you will nearly always change these settings. This is particularly true when you have intentionally applied under- or overexposure, for example when photographing a silhouette or when bracketing exposures.

White balance (WB)

The WB setting allows you to alter the white balance recorded in-camera. There is a drop-down menu with preset values that are similar to those found on the camera (*Daylight, Cloudy, Shade, Tungsten, Fluorescent, Flash,* and *Custom*). Click through these to see how different settings affect the image. The *As Shot* setting reverts to the setting applied in-camera. The *Auto* setting is Photoshop's best guess at the appropriate white balance, and not necessarily that of the camera.

There are also two sliders that can be used independently or in conjunction with the preset values. The *Temperature* slider sets the bias between yellow and blue. Moving the slider to the right will increase yellow (effectively warming the image, as when using an 81-series optical filter in the field), while shifting the slider to the left will increase the level of blue (cooling the image as when using an 80-series optical filter in the field). To gauge the effect of the *Temperature* slider, make exaggerated adjustments before settling on the optimal setting.

The *Tint* slider controls the bias between magenta (slide to the right) and green (slide to the left). A possible application for this control is to manage color shifts between natural-looking skin tones (magenta) and the vivid natural colors of nature (green). Again, experiment with different settings before settling on a preference.

Exposure, Shadows, and Brightness

Together, these three controls act like the *Levels* control in Photoshop, with *Exposure* controlling the white point, *Shadows* the black point, and *Brightness* the mid-tone point. With all three the histogram will change dynamically (when Preview is checked) to show the effects of any adjustments made.

Sliding the *Exposure* control right will lighten the image, while sliding the control left will darken it. Move the control to position the white point on the composite histogram close to the far right of the horizontal axis, avoiding clipping where possible.

By sliding the *Shadows* control to the left the image lightens, while sliding the control to the right darkens the image. Move the control to position the black point on the composite histogram close to the far left of the horizontal axis, avoiding clipping where possible.

Adjusting the *Brightness* control will lighten (right) or darken (left) the image without changing the black and white points. The *Recovery* slider is especially useful, allowing you to pull back detail lost in highlight areas.

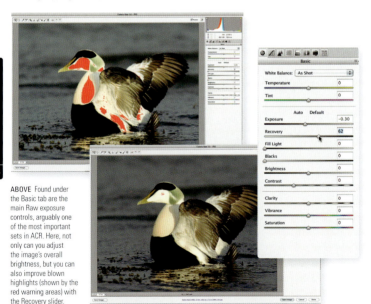

ABOVE Found under the Basic tab are the main Raw exposure controls, arguably one of the most important sets in ACR. Here, not only can you adjust the image's overall brightness, but you can also improve blown highlights (shown by the red warning areas) with the Recovery slider.

Contrast and Saturation

Adjusting contrast using the *Contrast* control will alter all the pixels to increase tonal range. It is the global nature of the adjustments that make this a less than satisfactory method of managing contrast and, as such, it's best to make only very slight adjustments, if necessary, and opt to process contrast using the *Curves* tool in Photoshop, where select adjustments can be made.

Like the *Contrast* control, the *Saturation* control in ACR applies any adjustments globally to all colors and all pixels. Again, my advice is to leave this setting alone and manage saturation in Photoshop itself.

Tone Curve

Under the second tab you'll find Adobe Camera Raw's interpretation of the *Curves* tool—a Photoshop mainstay. Here, however, two alternatives are offered; parametric and the traditional point curve. The latter will be covered later, but the parametric approach—introduced in Lightroom—is younger and works differently.

In either case the shades of the image are remapped so that lights become lighter or darker, midtones lighter or darker, and so on. This is represented by a curve; no change produces a straight line from the bottom left to the top right. The left end of the line represents dark tones, the right end highlights. Moving the line above the perfectly straight corner-to-corner diagonal lightens those tones, and pushing it below darkens them.

When you're working with parametric curves (you can choose alternative methods via the tabs beneath the *Tone Curve* pane's title bar), you do not work on the curve directly, but begin by moving the sliders beneath the graph to lighten or darken the respective tonal areas. The curve above will be redrawn to reflect the change (the gray area beneath is a histogram of the source image).

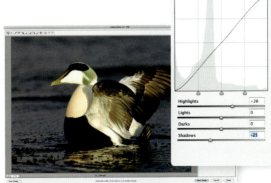

RIGHT The *Tone Curve* control works in a similar way to *Curves* in Photoshop. A very powerful tool, it allows selective contrast adjustment in an image. Here a very gentle "S" curve has been applied, increasing the overall contrast of the image very slightly.

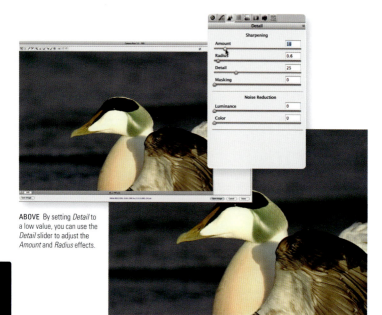

ABOVE By setting *Detail* to a low value, you can use the *Detail* slider to adjust the *Amount* and *Radius* effects.

Once you've adjusted the lower sliders to your satisfaction, you can now refine your changes by moving the goalposts that are the boundaries between the areas defined as highlights, lights, darks, and shadows. Do this by carefully moving the sliders directly beneath the histogram.

Detail

Next to the *Tone Curve* tab is *Detail*, under which are found the various *Sharpening* sliders. The *Amount* slider, which is set at a default of 25, controls the strength of the sharpening effect. The *Radius* slider's default setting is 1.0. As with the *Unsharp Mask* setting in Photoshop, this determines how many

pixels from an edge are sharpened. The *Detail* slider increases contrast in areas of the image where edges are prominent. Finally the *Masking* slider works by isolating the edges in the image. Moving the slider to the right ensures that sharpening is only applied to the edges of the image. Under *Noise Reduction*, *Luminance* helps reduce luminance noise, which shows as variations in brightness within tones, while *Color* helps reduce noise that often appears as random-color pixels in darker tones. If you need to use these tools, it is best to use them with the image enlarged to 100 percent on your screen, so you can monitor the effect closely.

HSL/Grayscale

This tab provides comprehensive control over the *Hue*, *Saturation*, and *Luminance* of eight ranges of color—reds, oranges, yellows, greens, aquas, blues, purples, and magentas. If all the colors are looking right in your image, except yellow, which is too vibrant, you can reduce it in the *Saturation* tab. Hue alters the color, from blue to purple, for example, while *Luminance* affects the brightness of the selected color range.

Clicking the *Convert to Grayscale* button will convert the image to black and white. You can then fine tune the conversion using the sliders; make a blue sky a darker tone, for example, or green leaves lighter.

Split Toning is used primarily with a grayscale image, allowing you to introduce very subtle color tones in which shadows and highlights are two separate colors.

BELOW The *HSL/Grayscale* tab allows for very fine control over color balance, essential if color fidelity is paramount. The *Convert to Grayscale* button creates a black and white version of the image and provides excellent levels of control over all the tones present.

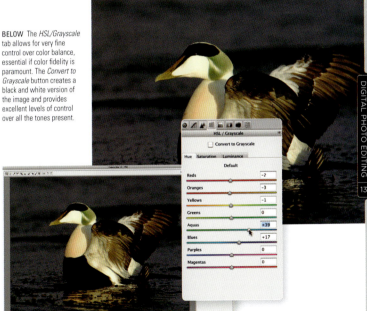

ABOVE The *Lens Corrections* tab corrects color fringing caused by chromatic aberration, a form of distortion in a lens. This is most noticeable in the high-contrast edge areas of an image.

Lens corrections

Found under this tab are the *Chromatic Aberration* and *Vignetting* sliders, but if you use decent lenses you may never have to use these tools. Chromatic aberration is color fringing, often caused by older lenses, while vignetting is the darkening of the corners of an image, often caused by using a wide-angle lens not designed for that particular DSLR.

Healing

As I've said before, there is little sense making extensive use of the rudimentary healing tools offered in Camera Raw when your next step is going to be a program with the power of Photoshop, but there are benefits to highlighting image flaws, especially dust spots that will appear in the same place in a whole series of images.

The procedure is simple, and it doesn't change the pixels of the Raw file. Instead the computer just records the target area (the spot) and the location of a suitable replacement area. With the *Retouch* tool selected and *Healing* mode selected, click once on the spot and then, if necessary, drag the green and white outlined circle which shows the source area. This should be moved to a clean area of the image which has a similar texture. You can click on as many marks as you like and give each a different source location.

...aw, and Photoshop
...ions available in
...have a parallel in
...on tool Lightroom
...underlying image
...All changes are non-
...that are processed
...her than applied to
...in a separate
...mera Raw saves
...nd applies them as

it hands a copy of the file over to Photoshop (at which point it ceases to be Raw).

All that said, many of the changes have parallels in Photoshop proper, and will be covered alongside those later in the book. It is up to you at which stage to make the changes, but it is logical to make wider ones in Camera Raw (or better still Lightroom) and more specific ones later, when you have Photoshop's full range of features at your disposal.

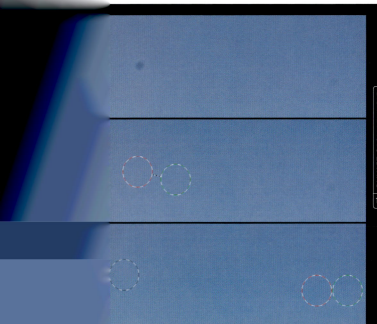

Improving Composition

Of course you want to get the composition of a photograph right when you are taking it, but sometimes due to a variety of factors such as focal length, this isn't possible. In these cases a little sensitive cropping in Photoshop can make all the difference. Cropping can also make a good composition even better.

Just about every photograph you'll ever take will benefit from a small amount of cropping. How to crop is very much down to individual taste, so think about composition and experiment with what feels pleasing to your eye. In most instances, if you are showing the whole bird in the picture, you need to give it room to breathe—cropping too tightly can be a big turnoff.

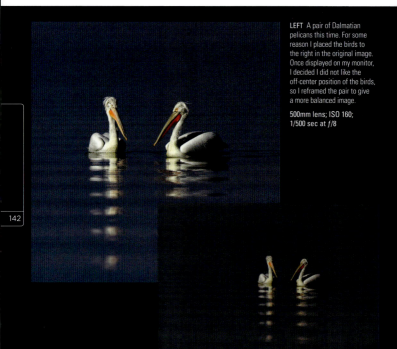

LEFT A pair of Dalmatian pelicans this time. For some reason I placed the birds to the right in the original image. Once displayed on my monitor, I decided I did not like the off-center position of the birds, so I reframed the pair to give a more balanced image.

500mm lens; ISO 160; 1/500 sec at f/8

You can crop your image inside the Raw converter or in Photoshop; whichever you choose, you will probably want to test cropping most images to see whether it improves the overall composition. It is, of course, better to take care to carefully frame and compose in the first instance, when photographing. If you rely on improving your composition with the *Crop* tool in Photoshop, you are immediately discarding some of the image, thus making the overall file size smaller. This can be a major drawback, as it will limit how much you can enlarge your image before it pixellates.

I regularly crop images into the panoramic format if I feel this is warranted. This is particularly useful if your bird is fairly small in the frame and there is a lot of uninteresting

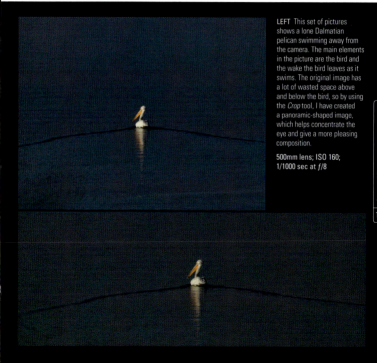

LEFT This set of pictures shows a lone Dalmatian pelican swimming away from the camera. The main elements in the picture are the bird and the wake the bird leaves as it swims. The original image has a lot of wasted space above and below the bird, so by using the *Crop* tool, I have created a panoramic-shaped image, which helps concentrate the eye and give a more pleasing composition.

500mm lens; ISO 160; 1/1000 sec at *f*/8

space above and below the bird; by cropping in this way you can place emphasis on your subject while retaining background interest.

Take a look at the examples of the crops on these pages: you will soon get a feel for what looks right. Cropping can be a fun part of post-processing, particularly when you experiment and find a crop that suddenly elevates your image to a far better picture than the one you started with.

Pro tip

When cropping a picture, experiment with different crops and don't be afraid to be radical sometimes. If your file size is big enough, try cropping in on the head of a large bird, or perhaps another part of the bird, to create a more abstract image. If you wish to sell your work, then keep your cropping to a minimum; one of the biggest causes of designers discarding images is too-tight crops, giving them little room to play with when fitting a page design over an image.

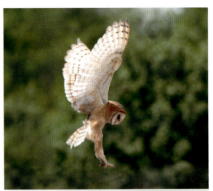

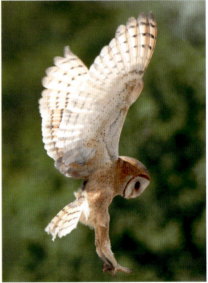

RIGHT Another time you may want to crop an image is to show how an image looks in a different format. This image of a barn owl was cropped into a portrait format.

RIGHT AND BELOW
This arctic tern is looking left, while to its right there is too much empty space to allow the picture to feel balanced. Therefore a simple crop to remove some of this superfluous space immediately improves the image.

70–200mm zoom lens; ISO 125; 1/800 sec at f/7.1

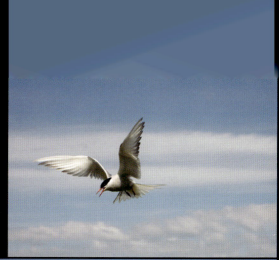

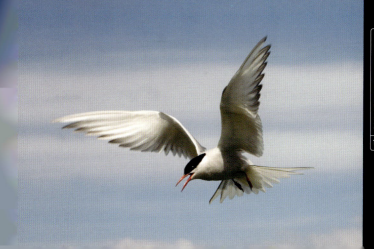

Adjusting Exposure, Contrast, and Color

Exposure, contrast, and color are the first basic adjustments to be made to an image in the computer. To avoid manipulating an image only to find that you can't start again, always keep an untouched master copy of the original.

If you are not shooting in Raw, then you will want to make your basic adjustments in Photoshop (or another image-editor of your choice) and the main one you may wish to make will be improving a poor exposure. As with many actions in Photoshop, there are various ways of doing this. If you are dealing with a JPEG, the first thing you should do is make a copy, so you have a master copy to fall back on if your experiments turn out badly.

When making corrections in image-editing software, you should always work in layers. A layer is a way of placing a filter over the surface of your image, so that when you

make adjustments you can see the difference you are making but the pixels in your image are not physically altered. This means you can do any number of adjustments in whichever layer you choose at any time without being destructive to the building blocks of the

BELOW Here we have an image of a black guillemot that is slightly too dark: I have underexposed by a third or half a stop. The levels palette is my first port of call—this shows the pixels bunched in the center and to the left, and there's a gap between the pixels and the edge of the histogram. Because the histogram does not meet the slider on the right, this means the contrast is low, so we need to increase this by dragging the slider in to the start of the histogram. You can see the improvement that has been made in the next screen shot opposite.

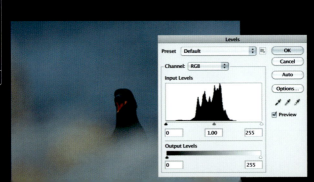

image. Once you have made all your adjustments in layers, you will have a big file due to the extra layers added to the original image. To reduce the file back to its native size you must remember to flatten the image by clicking *Layers > Flatten*.

Under *Layer > New Adjustment Layer*, there is a drop-down menu from which you can choose various options. Try and steer clear of *Brightness* and *Contrast*, as all adjustments you make with these tools risk compromising image quality, since they work rather crudely. If you are working in Photoshop rather than Elements, it is far better to make these adjustments using the *Curves* command.

Levels makes a good starting point. This allows contrast, color, and image brightness to be adjusted by using a simple slider. The *Levels* palette illustrates, by way of a histogram, the distribution of pixels across

the entire tonal range from black on the left to white on the right. This function is like the histogram found on the back of your camera when you check for exposure, the difference being that you can adjust these histograms. Contrast and exposure can be fine-tuned in *Levels* by means of the triangular sliders arranged along the bottom of the histogram. Your aim is to spread the tonal values in the image as much as possible; if you set the

BELOW Dragging both sliders to the start of the histogram and playing around with the middle slider has both brightened the image a little and improved the contrast, but it's still not quite as I want it. I'd like to make the background lighter.

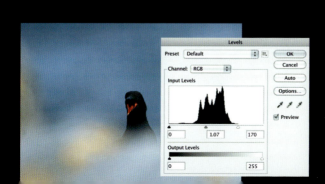

brightest pixel to white and the darkest pixel to black you will increase the amount of image contrast you have to work with without losing any information. To do this, move the sliders on either end in to meet the start of the graph. To make an accurate adjustment and to avoid clipping, hold down Alt (Opt)—the screen will go black for the *Shadows* slider and white for the *Highlights*. When moving the sliders in, stop as soon as you see clipping occurring in the form of the bright blue and red areas appearing. Once this has been done, you can brighten or darken the image using the middle slider.

You can make even more subtle adjustments to colors in *Levels* by clicking on the drop-down menu under *Channel*. Individual colors—red, green, and blue—can

then be adjusted individually, perhaps to correct for a color cast, for example, or to match a specific color. Color can also be adjusted in *Hue/Saturation*, but be careful not to overdo adjustments with this tool and create an unnatural-looking image.

BELOW To complete th[...] adjustment and make t[...] background lighter with[...] affecting the subject—[...] order for the bird to sta[...] out more—I have gone [...] the *Curves* palette. For [...] on *Curves* see page 15[...]

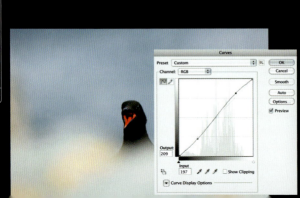

Pro tip

This great tinamou, photographed along the famous Pipeline Road in Panama, just needed some minor corrections. I increased the contrast and lightened the whole image a little by using the *Curves* tool, then made a minor color adjustment. The changes are subtle but they improve the overall feel of the image.

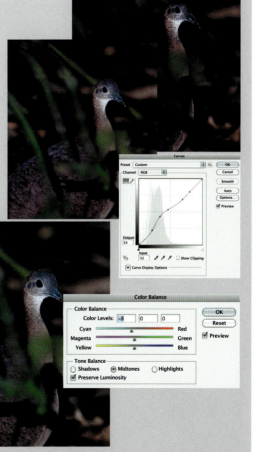

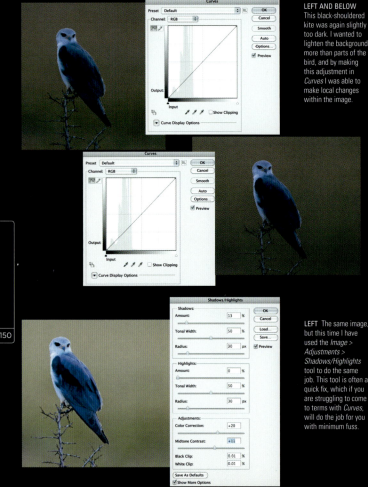

LEFT AND BELOW
This black-shouldered kite was again slightly too dark. I wanted to lighten the background more than parts of the bird, and by making this adjustment in *Curves* I was able to make local changes within the image.

LEFT The same image, but this time I have used the *Image > Adjustments > Shadows/Highlights* tool to do the same job. This tool is often a quick fix, which if you are struggling to come to terms with *Curves*, will do the job for you with minimum fuss.

150

RIGHT Using the *Brightness/Contrast* tool (*Image > Adjustments > Brightness/Contrast*) is often not the best way to brighten or increase the contrast in a picture, because these tools are rather crude compared to using *Curves*, where you can make more local adjustments. However, having said this, using the tool in small doses can be the answer to making a needed improvement.

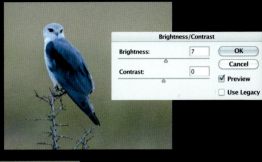

LEFT Another tool that should only be used in small doses, the *Hue/Saturation* (*Image > Adjustments > Hue/Saturation*) tool, is useful for helping to pump up an image's colors a little.

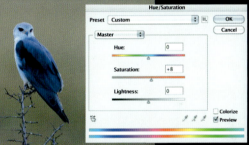

RIGHT You are unlikely to need to use the Color Balance tool (*Image > Adjustments > Color Balance*) very often. But, if you decide you have a color cast, or want to subtly adjust the colors in part of an image, then you can experiment with this palette.

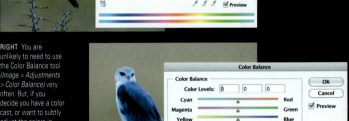

Using Curves

The *Levels* histogram is the first stop for checking brightness and contrast in an image; *Curves* is the second and by far the most powerful. Used with care and (admittedly) a lot of practice, it will become an invaluable tool.

Using *Curves* can seem like a daunting proposition, and of all the adjustment tools in Photoshop, it is perhaps the hardest to master. However, it is a very powerful application, and well worth getting to know. Individual tonal values and brightness and

contrast can be adjusted in *Curves*. The default graph displays a straight line running from dark tones in the bottom left to light tones in the top right.

Play around in *Curves* at first to see the effects created by dragging the line up for lightening the image and down for darkening it. Shadows can be darkened or lightened by moving the bottom of the line; conversely, the same effect can be made with the highlights at the top.

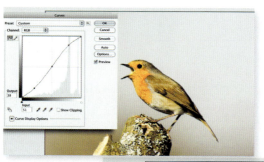

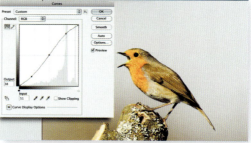

LEFT AND BELOW The image of this singing robin was a little flat, so I have added contrast to the midtones in *Curves* by plotting some holding points and then carefully adjusting the tonal areas of the picture I wanted to target. The result is this shallow S curve, which is typical of an increased midtone contrast.

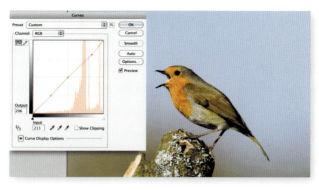

To target your adjustments, you need to plot a few holding points down your line: where you place these depends on which tones you wish to adjust. Your curve will commonly result in a shallow S shape. This lessens the contrast in the highlights and shadows while increasing contrast in the midtones. By creating this curve you can often enhance detail and give your image a bit of punch. Of course, not all images are going to need this treatment, and you might be able to create the desired effect in *Levels*. What *Curves* does give is added control—the more you use it, the more efficient you will become at making the very best of your images.

Finally, mention should be made of the *Shadows/Highlights* tool in Photoshop. This can be an excellent alternative to fiddling around in *Curves* and is very useful to bird photographers since it helps bring out detail in both shadow and highlight areas. However, overdoing the use of this tool will result in nasty halos or a very flat image overall; like all adjustment tools in Photoshop, the bottom line is always to trust your judgment.

ABOVE In the original image the sky was pale, with very little color. By adjusting the individual color channels accessed in the drop-down menu, I was able to plot some holding points before adjusting the color of the sky (represented as the light tones at the top of the graph) to color it blue.

Pro tip

If you want to make very localized adjustments to your image, hold down your mouse button and the cursor will become an eyedropper when you move it over your image. The corresponding point will be shown on the *Curves* graph wherever you place the eyedropper. Therefore, if you have an area of the picture you want left alone, you can place anchor points to protect it.

The Clone Stamp and Healing Brush

However clean you keep your camera's sensor, it is inevitable that specks of dust will find their way onto it. This creates blemishes on the image, which can be very obtrusive. These two tools can be used to repair and improve images.

Dust is the digital photographer's greatest enemy, and no matter how careful you are, you will end up with dust on your sensor, causing dust spots to appear on your images. These need to be removed by either the *Clone Stamp* or one of the *Healing Brush* tools.

Although they do the same job, these two tools differ in how they work. The *Clone Stamp* works by selecting an area adjacent to the spot you wish to remove, and then stamping that sampled piece of the image over the offending spot. You sample by first selecting a brush size—either by using the square

brackets on your keyboard or from the brush palette—and then choosing the area you wish to clone from. Click Alt (Opt) and then place your brush over the spot for cloning.

If you are doing a lot of cloning, whether that involves removing multiple dust spots or an obtrusive background feature, then take care over where you clone from, so that you do not leave an obvious trail of cloned patches. Done properly, your work should ideally be undetectable.

The *Healing Brush* is often the superior choice when cloning out dust spots. Where the *Clone Stamp* wins is in areas of sharply contrasting edges, such as on the plumage of a bird or a critical piece of background. The *Healing Brush* works in much the same way as the *Clone Stamp*, but copies the texture of the source. Since Photoshop CS2, the *Spot Healing*

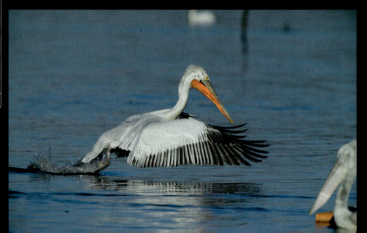

Pro tip

Many photographers use the *Clone Stamp* to put catchlights in a bird's eyes, by sampling a pale or highlighted area with the desired size of stamp. A far more subtle way of placing a catchlight is to use the *Dodge* tool: by picking up any lighter tones in the eye, you can create a more subtly pleasing effect.

Brush needs no sampling; all you need do is place the cursor over the offending area and click—this is great for speed when eradicating dust spots from areas of sky or water.

When eradicating dust spots, you need to be zoomed in to 100 percent (double-click on the *Magnify* tool), then systematically work your way across the image. I start in the top left corner and gradually move to the bottom right, covering the whole image accurately. When using the stamps, the brushes need to be reasonably hard—the more detailed the area to be cloned, the harder the brush should be. The *Healing Brush* should never be soft, as this prevents the healing function.

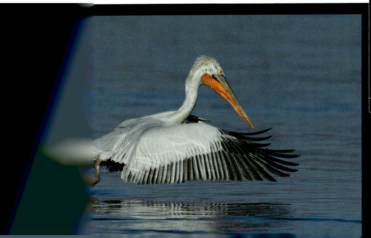

Resizing and Output Formats

Both the most popular formats for digital cameras, JPEGs and Raw files, can be enlarged to make bigger images. This can be done in Photoshop or by using one of the many third-party plug-ins available; both produce similar results.

There may occasionally be times when your file size is not big enough to produce a large print. The answer is to add more pixels to the image to enlarge the file size. This process is called interpolation.

A badly prepared file will interpolate poorly, as any imperfections in the image will be magnified, therefore it is good practice to optimize your image as best you can. When shooting in Raw and knowing the size of file you will need, you can interpolate before entering Photoshop. If working with a JPEG

or processed TIFF file, you need to do this in Photoshop or with a third-party plug-in—a number of options are available, with the most popular being Genuine Fractals. I have compared Genuine Fractals with the bicubic method available in Photoshop, and I can see no advantage. There has been a long-standing school of thought that advises interpolating by using a step method, enlarging by 10 percent or so each time, but this has now been proven to give poorer results than interpolating in just one step.

To interpolate in Photoshop, go to *Image > Image Size*; then, starting at the bottom, check the three boxes. The drop-down menu next to *Resample Image* gives the algorithm options for resizing: *Bicubic Sharper* can be used to reduce a file size, for enlarging you should use

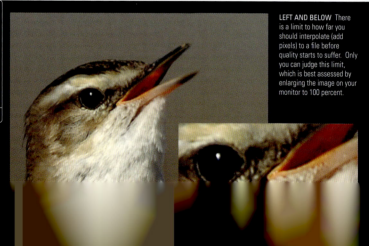

LEFT AND BELOW There is a limit to how far you should interpolate (add pixels) to a file before quality starts to suffer. Only you can judge this limit, which is best assessed by enlarging the image on your monitor to 100 percent.

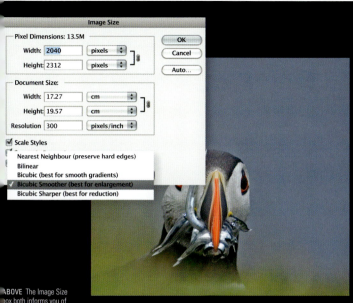

Image Size		
Pixel Dimensions: 13.5M		OK
Width: 2040	pixels	Cancel
Height: 2312	pixels	Auto...
Document Size:		
Width: 17.27	cm	
Height: 19.57	cm	
Resolution 300	pixels/inch	

☑ Scale Styles

Nearest Neighbour (preserve hard edges)
Bilinear
Bicubic (best for smooth gradients)
✓ Bicubic Smoother (best for enlargement)
Bicubic Sharper (best for reduction)

ABOVE The Image Size box both informs you of the picture's size and dimensions, and allows you to either reduce or increase the size of your image. To do this, either increase or decrease the number of pixels or change a value under Document Size. Change one value, and the others will automatically adjust. When enlarging an image you should have all three boxes at the bottom checked off, and choose one of the algorithms (processes) listed in the drop-down menu under Bicubic. When interpolating (enlarging), choose Bicubic Smoother for the best results.

Pro tip

Remember never to sharpen the image before interpolating. By doing so, artifacts (imperfections) created by sharpening will be magnified, which may lead to a noticeable loss in image quality.

Bicubic Smoother. Above are the *Document Size* values and *Pixel Dimensions*; changing the value in one box will automatically adjust the values in the other, so you need to change one of the sets of values for your enlargement.

Finally, if you have been working with a JPEG, you are likely to want to save your image as a JPEG. If you have been working from a Raw file, to retain the best quality, you should save your image as a TIFF. Click *File > Save As*—this gives you the option of changing your file name and allows you to choose a location to save the image in, and in which format. The latter gives a drop-down menu from which you click your selection. If saving as a JPEG, you will be given a further option of choosing a quality setting.

Sharpening

There are more theories about sharpening than almost anything else in digital photography. Experts have different ideas on the best way to sharpen, and you should review what they do, but there is no substitute for experimenting yourself.

All digital images need some amount of sharpening before being printed. Sharpening should be your last act before output, and ideally no or very little sharpening should have been applied either in your camera or in Photoshop. The reason for this is that sharpening will introduce artifacts that degrade the picture, but these will not be visible if sharpening at the end of the work flow and if you do not oversharpen. If you were to sharpen before making color adjustments and retouching, these artifacts would be accentuated; even worse is sharpening before resizing or interpolating the image.

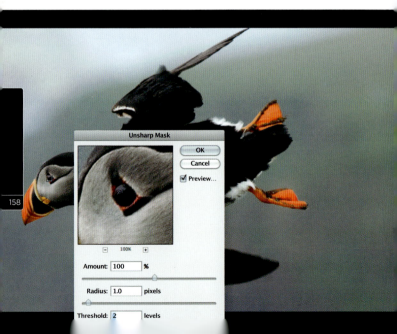

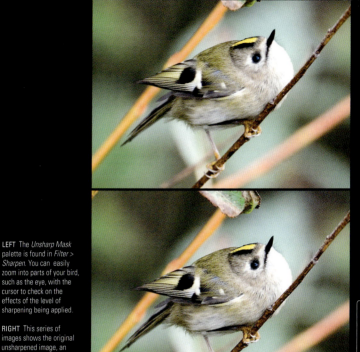

LEFT The *Unsharp Mask* palette is found in *Filter > Sharpen*. You can easily zoom into parts of your bird, such as the eye, with the cursor to check on the effects of the level of sharpening being applied.

RIGHT This series of images shows the original unsharpened image, an image sharpened an optimum amount, and an image that has been oversharpened. Sharpening is more of an art than a science; you may feel the need to experiment a little to refine your judgment on how much each image will need for the desired output.

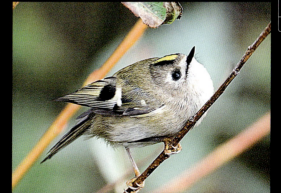

Sharpening effectively boosts contrast along edges in the image, which is why when you increase an image's contrast it appears to become sharper. You cannot sharpen a picture that was not in sharp focus in the first place, because the extra detail looked for was never initially captured in the photograph.

The various sharpening tools are found under *Filter* in Photoshop. There are two that are relevant: the *Unsharp Mask* (USM) filter has traditionally been the tool to use, and Photoshop now also features *Smart Sharpen*, which gives the option of sharpening shadow and highlight areas of the image separately.

Whether using *Unsharp Mask* or *Smart Sharpen*, or sharpening tools in other software, remember that sharpening is very subjective. I see many prints where the sharpening has been overdone, while pictures are often published where clearly not enough sharpening has been applied. The sharpening effect you see on the screen will not necessarily translate to the same degree on your print—this difference is even more pronounced when images are published, as the preparation of an image for press creates a loss in sharpness. Because sharpening is not a science, you need to experiment; once experienced in the art, you will be able to judge the level of sharpening required for your proposed output.

The amount to sharpen in percentage terms will vary from image to image, but typically I never go above 200 percent. The *Radius* and *Threshold* settings affect the distribution of sharpening. The *Radius* affects the area by the increased contrast—a setting between 1 and 2 should be sufficient here. *Threshold* measures contrast between pixels—the higher you go, the less your image sharpens. Again, you need to experiment for the effect you desire.

High Pass sharpening

A less convenient but in many ways a more effective method of sharpening than using the *Unsharp Mask* is to utilize Photoshop's *High Pass* filter. This has the benefit of restricting the sharpening effect to the edges in an image.

1) Open the image you want to sharpen.

2) Duplicate the background layer and call it "High Pass."

3) With the *High Pass* layer selected change the *Blending Mode* to *Overlay*.

4) Go to *Filter > Other > High Pass* to run the *High Pass* filter. Check the *Preview* box and set the *Radius* slider so that you are sharpening just the fine detail in the image.

5) Turn the *High Pass* layer on and off to view the effect of the sharpening. Additionally, you can fine tune the level of sharpening by reducing the *Opacity* slider in the Layers palette.

Smart Sharpen

As sophisticated as Photoshop's *Unsharp Mask* is, the main drawback is that it applies more or less the same level of sharpening over the entire image, when what we really want to do is restrict sharpening to the areas that really improve the look of the image—the edges. *Smart Sharpen* can help localize the effect of sharpening in two ways. First there is the *Remove* menu. While the *Gaussian Blur* works in much the same way as the standard *Unsharp Mask*, selecting *Lens Blur* applies sharpening to a narrower radius, which helps with images that have very fine detail, such as a bird's feathers. Use *Smart Sharpen* with *Lens Blur* selected and you'll achieve more subtle sharpening. The other benefit of *Smart Sharpen* over *Unsharp*

Mask is that there are *Shadow* and *Highlight* tabs that allow you to make fine adjustments to the level of sharpening in these two key tonal areas. Over sharpening highlight areas can cause small highlight regions to blow out—very ugly. While sharpening shadows will attract unwanted attention to shadow areas. Under each tab you'll find a *Fade Amount* slider—increasing the value reduces the sharpening effect in those specific tones; a *Tonal Width Slider*—which determines which specific tones are affected by the *Fade Amount* slider; and the *Radius* slider—which includes a greater number of pixels in the tonal area. Together these controls provide you with much more flexibility when sharpening images.

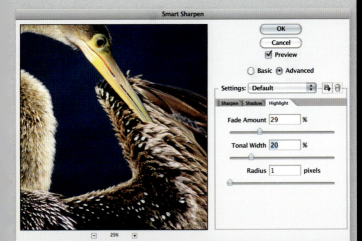

Printing

The prices of inkjet color printers have tumbled over the years, but don't be tempted to buy the cheapest available, as the results will look cheap, too. You want the best for your images, so get the best you can afford.

Printing your bird pictures at home on your desktop is a great way to enjoy your growing photography skills and, of course, the birds you have seen. There are many inkjet printers on the market, with perhaps the best-known made by Epson, Canon, and Hewlett Packard. All these manufacturers produce excellent machines, and which to buy is very much a personal choice.

One factor that will govern your choice of printer is how large you want your prints to be. Many compacts and most DSLRs are perfectly capable of producing Tabloid/A3 (approximately 16 x 11-in) prints; although you may not necessarily want large prints all the time, it's nice to have the option should you really want to show off a particular image, and of course A3 printers can print on smaller paper sizes, not just A3.

Inkjet printers work by spraying droplets of ink onto paper that are so small they are indiscernible to the naked eye. Generally speaking, the bigger the prints you want to make, the bigger the machine and the more this will cost. While lower-cost machines usually have four colors, the more expensive

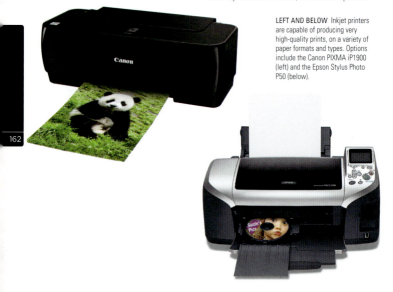

LEFT AND BELOW Inkjet printers are capable of producing very high-quality prints, on a variety of paper formats and types. Options include the Canon PIXMA iP1900 (left) and the Epson Stylus Photo P50 (below).

Image Size

Pixel Dimensions: 36.4M

Width: 2912 pixels

Height: 4368 pixels

OK

Cancel

Auto...

Document Size:

Width: 30.82 cm

Height: 46.23 cm

Resolution: 240 pixels/inch

☑ Scale Styles
☑ Constrain Proportions
☑ Resample Image

Bicubic (best for smooth gradients)

LEFT Photoshop's Image Size dialog box is where you can set the output resolution for your image. For printing you should set Resolution to between 240–300 pixels/inch (ppi). This figure should not be confused with an inkjet printer's resolution, which is measured in dots per inch (dpi).

and larger machines use six or seven colors— more accurately, they add tones such as light gray and pale versions of cyan and magenta. These machines give you improved, smoother tonal gradations. That said, many of these subtle differences may not be readily discernible to the average viewer, particularly in images of birds.

Printers are relatively cheap to buy; your major costs will be paper and ink. If you intend to do a lot of printing, you might want to look at the various options for ink: some printers have just one cartridge supplying all the colors, some have individual color cartridges, and others still have cartridges that can be refilled with ink. Your choice will be down to economics, but pigmented inks will give you the best life expectancy when matched with archival papers. Which kind of paper you choose is down to personal preference. Canvas is currently very popular, as are fine-art watercolor papers, or you can go for more traditional matte or gloss paper.

Printer resolution and image resolution are often confused. Printer resolution is how the ink is put down on the paper, expressed as dots per inch (dpi). A resolution of 1440 x 720dpi will give excellent results. Image resolution, on the other hand, is made up of the pixels per inch in your image and is referred to as ppi (this is often referred to incorrectly as dpi). For the best results when printing, a figure of 240–300ppi should be used. This figure can be set in *Image > Image Size* in Photoshop.

The file size of your image needs to be large enough for the size of print you plan to produce, if you want to get the best quality print possible. Prints produced too large for their file size may appear acceptable, but the chances are that they could be improved by using the correct file size. As a simple guide, a good 8 x 10 inch print needs a file size of 15–20Mb. If you have a digiscoped image, for example, with a 12Mb file, you will need to interpolate a little for the best result.

Although printmaking is an art rather than a science, you should aim to remove as much of the guesswork from it as possible. Strive for accuracy in producing a print that closely matches the image displayed on your monitor by calibrating both your monitor and printer. As with your monitor, your printer needs an ICC profile so it can accurately interpret the color information being sent to it by your computer. Printers have generic profiles that are often adequate, and if the prints you produce are a decent enough match for your needs, you might not feel the need to do any more. Far more accurate are printer profiles that match printers with specific paper combinations; these can be bought off the

ORIGINAL COLORS

HIGH-RESOLUTION HALFTONES

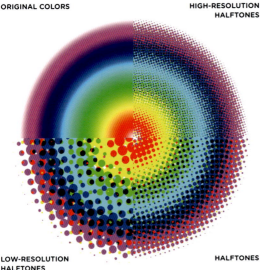

LOW-RESOLUTION HALFTONES

HALFTONES

LEFT This diagram shows how all colors are created from four separate colors—cyan, magenta, yellow, and black—on a traditional printing press. Most inkjets use alternative psuedo-random dithering patterns to distribute dots.

ABOVE Making prints of your photos can be very rewarding. I converted this image of a barn owl from color to black and white. You can do this in Photoshop by discarding all the color information to convert to a grayscale image; however, this can give a flat, very gray-looking result. For a punchier conversion, go to *Layer > New Adjustment Layer > Black & White*. You can play around with the sliders for your desired effect.

164

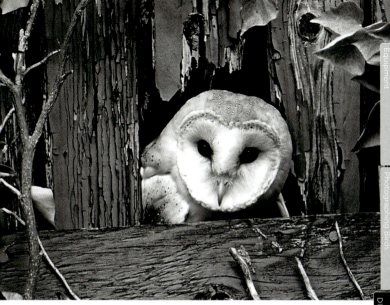

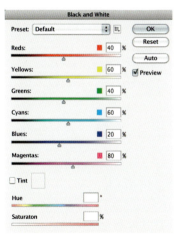

Internet. You can take this a step further and create a custom profile or get a profiling service to do this for you. Once your printer is profiled with the inks and paper you use, you should get consistent results, as your printer and monitor will be talking the same color language, so to speak.

One common problem you may encounter when using inkjet printers is clogging of the printer head, which can cause lines or very odd colors to appear. This may be caused by the use of third-party inks; in addition these inks will not be of a high quality, and chances are the colors on your print will not be as accurate as they could have been—saving money on inks is normally a false economy. Heads can be cleaned either by the printer utility within the printer's software, or in some models by pressing a button on the front of the printer—see your manual for details.

Getting Published

Whether you use a compact camera for digiscoping or a DSLR, there is no reason why a good bird image should not be acceptable for publication. There is a lot of competition, however, and you need to be able and willing to get your work seen.

There are very few enthusiastic photographers who take pictures and who do not have an ambition to have their work published in one form or another. There was a time when many bird magazines, particularly in Great Britain, had most of their images supplied by a few dedicated bird photographers. The boom in digital bird photography, and particularly in digiscoping, has changed all that: open any bird magazine today, and you will see a multitude of different names sprinkled throughout the picture credits.

Digiscoping rare birds has been the route into being published for many, since there is a constant hunger for images of newsworthy birds. The ease of photographing rarities by digiscope, however, means competition is fierce. I know of one bird magazine that, after a good weekend for rare birds in spring and fall, often receives over two hundred e-mailed images in a day!

While digiscoped images are fine for small reproductions in bird magazines, if you are serious about being published you need to shoot with a DSLR to produce the quality required. If you can write, great; magazine editors love features that have a strong pictorial content, and offering a complete package of words and pictures is an attractive proposition for editors, compared with offering just one or the other. There are some wildlife photographers who make a living by writing and supplying images to magazines—just don't expect to get rich.

Pro tip

If you send images out to potential clients to view, make sure everything you send is of a high standard. Initial impressions are crucial, and if you fail to make an impact at the first opportunity, chances are you will not be at the top of the list when a client goes looking for pictures. You should try to view your work objectively, and by only sending out your very best images, your chances of success will be increased.

LEFT Good shots of birds can be used in more than just books and magazines about birds. It's surprising the usage you can get from certain shots.

RIGHT Although there is not a huge market for images of specific bird species, there is a hunger for images that are generic in nature, and if they mirror human emotion, as with the examples shown on these pages, then they are suitable for all manner of uses, such as advertising, book covers, greeting cards, calendars, and jigsaws.

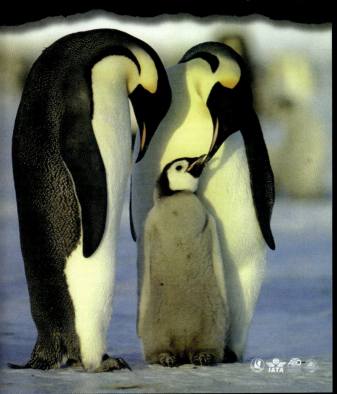

WILDLIFE
WORLDWIDE

Classic Tailored Wildlife Holidays

Equipment

Photographing Birds

DIGITAL PHOTO EDITING 167

Reference

IATA · AITO

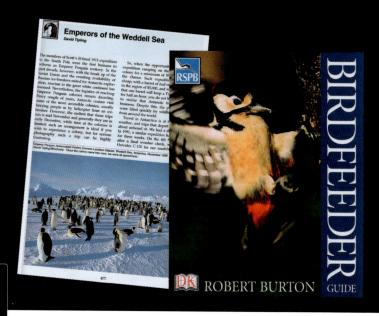

Emperors of the Weddell Sea
David Tipling

The members of Scott's ill-fated 1911 expedition to the South Pole were the first humans to witness an Emperor Penguin rookery. In the past decade, however, with the break up of the Soviet Union and the resulting availability of Russian ice-breakers suited for Antarctic exploration, tourism to the great white continent has boomed. Nevertheless, the logistics of reaching Emperor Penguin colonies remain daunting. Every couple of years, Antarctic cruises visit some of the more accessible colonies, usually ferrying people by helicopter from an ice-breaker. However, the earliest that these trips ran is mid November and generally they are in early December, while time at the colonies is limited; such an arrangement is ideal if you wish to experience a colony, but for serious photography such a trip can be highly frustrating.

So, when the opportunity [...] expedition camping on the [...] colony for a minimum of [...] the chance. Such expediti[...] cheap; with a barrel of fuel c[...] in the region of $5,000, and [...] that one barrel will keep a Tw[...] for half an hour, you do not h[...] to realise that Antarctic b[...] business. Despite this, the p[...] were filled quickly by wildlif[...] from around the world.

Travel in Antarctica is at t[...] weather, and trips that depart[...] about unheard of. We had 4 d[...] In 1991, a similar expedition h[...] for three weeks. On the 4th [...] after a final weather check, [...] Hercules C-130 for our southb[...]

Emperor Penguins *Aptenodytes forsteri*, Dawson-Lambton Glacier, Weddell Sea, Antarctica, November 1988
(David Tipling/Windrush) 'Once this colony came into view, we were all speechless.'

477

RSPB

DK ROBERT BURTON

BIRDFEEDER GUIDE

There are many other routes to selling your work. Note that I say "sell"—I would urge you never to give your work away for free, as this sets a bad precedent and you are simply allowing yourself to be taken advantage of. Photographs are valuable commodities that sell products, vacations, and most other things we consume in life. Be wary of tour operators inviting images to be sent for publication in their brochures—you may get the warm glow of seeing your work in print, but in reality your work will be devalued, as the use of it is just the cheap option for those businesses. Similarly, be wary of photographic competitions that hide away a clause giving them the right to use your pictures for anything and everything, forever, for nothing.

OPPOSITE Once you've amassed a good number of images—enough for an effective portfolio—consider creating your own website. It's possible to set one up relatively cheaply these days and it's a good way to get your work seen. You can also try selling prints from the site, though don't expect too much revenue from this route!

ABOVE Two further, perhaps more traditional, examples of where you might see your work being used—in bird magazines and books. If you have an interest in and aptitude for writing, you may find that offering your services as both a writer and photographer generates quite a lot of work.

david tipling photography

home   about me   gallery   latest news   picture of the week   tours and workshops   published work   portfolio   books   links   search   contact

Portfolio

The images on this page reflect the techniques David uses to capture images and gives a flavor of his distinctive style. The aim is always to make pictures that have a soul rather than just straight portraits of subjects. His aim is often to come up with new angles on familiar and not so familiar subjects both at home and abroad.

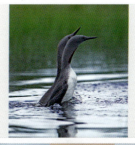

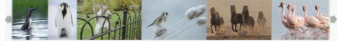

You may decide you want someone else to market your pictures for you, in which case you need an agent. Agents have big overheads that include a lot of promotion, running websites, and paying staff, so they typically take at least 50 percent from each sale they make for you. Having an agent does not guarantee lots of sales; the market for bird pictures is relatively small, especially for the more obscure species. Couple this with the flood of fantastic images being taken year after year, and there is plenty of competition.

To make sales, your work needs to stand out, and building a niche for yourself by developing a distinctive style or specialization will help. In my early days, I built up an extensive coverage of British garden birds and became well known for those images within the business.

As well as using agents, I market my own work quite aggressively, both through direct contact with potential clients and through a website. These have proliferated in recent years, and if you have a good site with plenty of images online to choose from, you are likely to get picture buyers using you regularly—too little choice means buyers are not likely to waste their time. To combat this problem, some photographers have joined together to promote their bird pictures on one common site, giving buyers a decent choice. This kind of cooperation is likely to increase in the future.

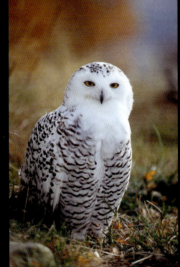

LEFT When taking images for publication, leave plenty of space around the bird. Cropping too tightly will reduce the chances of your picture being chosen, as designers often need surrounding space to accommodate other elements such as text and logos. With this image of a snowy owl looking at the camera, I have left space at the top of the frame for type. This would be ideal as a book or magazine cover because the bird is looking directly at the camera, engaging the viewer.

500mm lens; ISO 160; 1/500 sec at ƒ/8

LEFT A less expensive alternative to having your own website is to join one of the many online photography communities, such as Flickr. These hosting services often feature special interest groups where you can post images and share comments with like-minded photographers.

RIGHT Birdwatching is booming, with more and more people discovering it as a rewarding pursuit. As a result there are lots of opportunities to take images of people in the act of birdwatching.

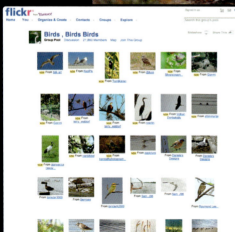

Entering competitions successfully is another way to see your images in print being enjoyed by a wide audience. The International Wild Bird Photographer of the Year is perhaps the best-known competition for bird photographers. Competitions are a big lottery however, as photography is so subjective that you cannot say definitively that one image is necessarily more aesthetically pleasing than another. We all have our individual tastes based on particular personal experience, so when choosing images for a competition, you can often be too close to your work to make an objective judgment. Show a set of images to family and friends, and if they consistently pick certain images as their favorites, the chances are these will be the pictures that appeal to the judges, too.

If you simply want to share your photos, you can have a Web site, or you can contribute to one of the many forums and Web sites devoted to birds on the Web. Surfbirds (www. surfbirds.com) is one of the best known and is particularly popular with digiscopers wanting to share images of rare birds. There are many others; often you can make good contacts through them, and they can be a source of very useful information, whether it be for good sites to photograph birds or simply for ideas on technique or equipment.

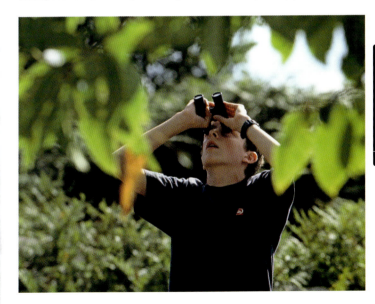

Long-term Picture Storage

You will have a lot of bird images to store, so a logical filing system is invaluable in helping you to find them again quickly. When storing images, as well as being easy to access, they also need to be secure, so keep them safely backed up on CDs or DVDs.

Deciding on how to store images for the long term will depend largely on how many you take and whether you shoot JPEGs or Raw—if you use the latter, you will need a lot more storage capacity than for the former.

When you store your images they need to be cataloged in some way, so that individual pictures can be found easily. There are many ways of doing this, and you need to think about the best system for you. Because I sometimes take hundreds of images a month,

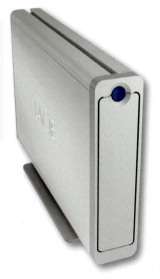

I file my images in folders under bird's names, which are then placed in folders titled with the relevant families. Thus, if I want to look at all my osprey images, for example, I can click on the "Birds of prey" folder, and within that the "Osprey" folder.

My images are stored on external hard drives that connect to the computer, and I keep two backup drives in case of failure, one of which is at another address. I go to great lengths to protect my images because they are my livelihood, but whatever the level of interest you have, you should have your images backed up at least once. Hard drives do fail, and if you do not back up, then you run the very real risk of losing everything.

The other option is to store your images online, or on CDs or DVDs. Longevity of these latter media has never been proved, as they have not yet been around for long enough. The safest option is to transfer your backed-up files from their CD or DVD format to new CDs or DVDs every five years or so, thus avoiding the media degenerating in the long term. If choosing disks for long-term storage, go for those that have gold in their dyes—gold does not degenerate very quickly and is reflective. Disks with poor reflective properties in their dyes are those that CD and DVD players struggle to read after a while. While CDs are restricted to 700Mb of data, a DVD will allow you to store around 4.2Gb of data, and so these are more suited to photographers who shoot in Raw.

LEFT Hard drives can be so small that they fit on your key ring. However, larger versions such as this LaCie model can hold hundreds of gigabytes (Gb) of data and are better value.

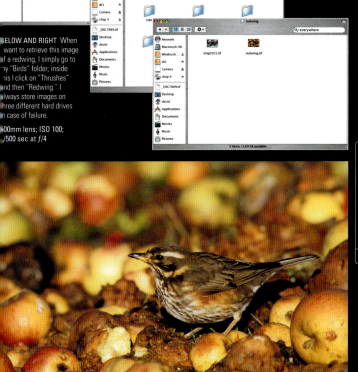

LEFT The process of filing and retrieving an image.

BELOW AND RIGHT When I want to retrieve this image of a redwing, I simply go to my "Birds" folder; inside this I click on "Thrushes" and then "Redwing." I always store images on three different hard drives in case of failure.

300mm lens; ISO 100;
1/500 sec at f/4

Bird Photography and Ethics

Hopefully, you photograph birds because you love and admire them, and want to translate this into recording their existence. Don't allow your enthusiasm or desire for the perfect picture to override either the honesty of your photographs or the welfare of your subjects.

The old saying "a photograph never lies" is now well and truly out of date. There was a time when wildlife images could be trusted as exact representations of a scene captured by the photographer. Now we have the means to composite images from many different pictures, to add extra birds or place a bird in a different setting—the imagination is really the only limit. "Photographic artist" is a name being increasingly used to describe photographers who regularly manipulate their images; and indeed, this practice is helping to develop wildlife photography as an accepted form of art.

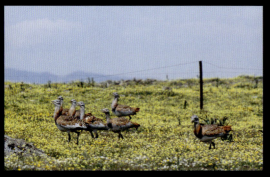

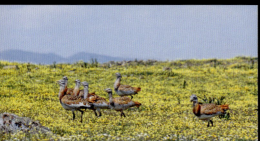

LEFT I see no problem with tidying up part of the background, as in this example of a flock of great bustards, where I have removed the fence and improved the colors. I would not, however, add birds to the image or materially change the scene without declaring this in the caption.

200mm lens; ISO 100; 1/500 sec at f/11

RIGHT Although not under immediate threat, the Atlantic Puffin is a protected species in some European countries—not including Iceland, where it is hunted by net and its heart eaten as a delicacy.

500mm lens; ISO 100; 1/500 sec at f/4

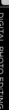

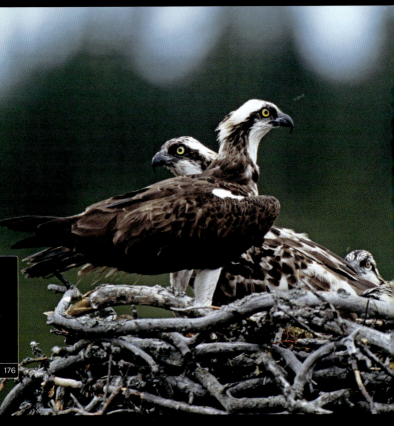

ABOVE A number of species are
legally protected against disturbance;
for example, it is illegal to photograph
ospreys in the nest in Great Britain
without a license. This image was
taken in Finland.

500mm lens; ISO 100; 1/350 sec at ƒ/8

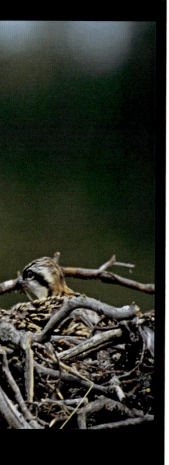

All digital images need some manipulation to color and other variables to optimize the shot; backgrounds can be tidied up or made more blurry, for example. Where the photographer does have a duty is in stating when an image has been materially altered to such an extent that it no longer represents the scene viewed at the time. Without such disclosure, how can we marvel at the natural world through the eyes of a photographer without wondering whether what we are viewing is reality? Some photographers argue that it is the end result that matters, and that how the image was made is immaterial. This is fine if your only consideration is the aesthetics of an image, but by not declaring that an image is a composite you are damaging the integrity of other wildlife photographers, as the viewing public can lose trust in whether an image is a true representation.

Although we do not have an official bird photographers' code, there are a number of points worth considering. It has been said many times but is worth saying again: the welfare of your subject should always come before the photograph. Hounding tired migrants or rarities leads to both photographers and birdwatchers getting a bad name. You should respect private land, particularly when it comes to erecting blinds. Nest photography these days is very much out of fashion, but if you do wish to photograph birds in a nest, some rules need to be observed: gardening around the nest should be kept to an absolute minimum, and if vegetation needs to be moved, then it should be tied back, not cut. Blinds should be moved into position slowly over a period of days, and photography should be abandoned if the birds you hope to photograph have an adverse reaction to any intrusion.

Many species require a license for photography of birds in or near the nest. You should be fully conversed in your country's legal requirements in this regard.

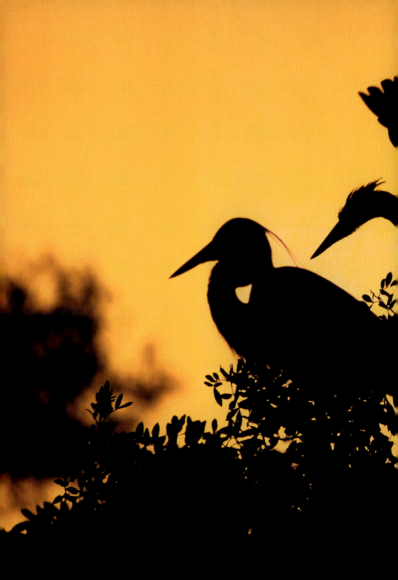

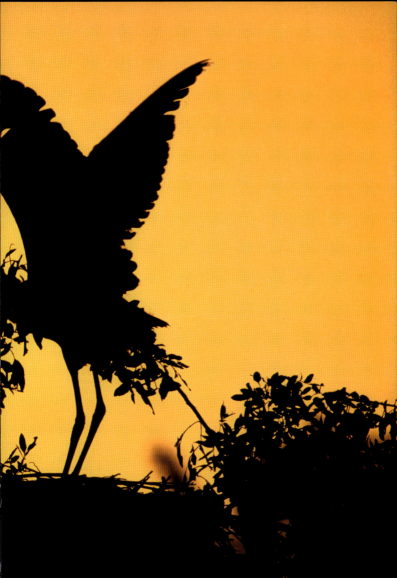

Glossary

APERTURE
The opening behind the camera lens through which light passes on its way to the image sensor (CCD/CMOS).

ARCHIVE
The process of organizing and saving digital images (or other files) for ready retrieval and research.

ARTIFACT
A flaw in a digital image.

BACKLIGHTING
The result of shooting with a light source, natural or artificial, behind the subject to create a silhouette or rim-lighting effect.

BIT (BINARY DIGIT)
The smallest data unit of binary computing, being a single 1 or 0.

BIT DEPTH
The number of bits of color data for each pixel in a digital image. A photographic-quality image needs eight bits for each of the red, green, and blue channels, making for a bit depth of 24.

BRACKETING
A method of ensuring a correctly exposed photograph by taking three shots; one with the supposed correct exposure, one slightly underexposed, and one slightly overexposed.

BRIGHTNESS
The level of light intensity. One of the three dimensions of color in the standard HSB color system. *See also* Hue and Saturation.

BUFFER
Temporary storage space in a camera, where images are held before processing and transfer to the camera's memory card.

BURST DEPTH
The number of images you can take before the camera's buffer fills and prevents you from taking any more.

BURST RATE
The number of frames the camera can take per second.

BYTE EIGHT BITS
The basic unit of desktop computing. 1,024 bytes equals one kilobyte (KB), 1,024 kilobytes equals one megabyte (MB), and 1,024 megabytes equals one gigabyte (GB).

CALIBRATION
The process of adjusting a device, such as a monitor, so that it works consistently with others, such as scanners or printers.

CCD (CHARGE-COUPLED DEVICE)
A tiny photocell used to convert light into an electronic signal. Used in densely packed arrays, CCDs are the recording medium used in some (the majority of cameras now use CMOS sensors) digital cameras.

CHANNEL
Part of an image as stored in the computer; similar to a layer. Commonly, a color image will have a channel allocated to each primary color (e.g. RGB) and sometimes one or more for a mask or other effects.

CLIPPING
The effect of losing detail in the lighter areas of your image because the exposure was long enough for the photosites to fill (and record maximum values).

CLIPPING PATH
The line used by desktop publishing software to cut an image from its background.

CLONING
In an image-editing program, the process of duplicating pixels from one part of an image to another.

CMOS (COMPLEMENTARY METAL-OXIDE SEMICONDUCTOR)
An alternative sensor technology to the CCD, CMOS chips are used in ultra-high-resolution cameras from most manufacturers.

CMYK (CYAN, MAGENTA, YELLOW, KEY)
The four process colors used for printing, including black (key).

COLOR GAMUT
The range of color that can be produced by an output device, such as a printer, a monitor, or a film recorder.

COLOR TEMPERATURE
A way of describing the color differences in light, measured in Kelvins and using a scale that ranges from dull red (1900 K), through orange, to yellow, white, and blue (10,000 K).

COMPRESSION
Technique for reducing the amount of space that a file occupies, by removing redundant data. There are two kinds of compression: standard and lossy. While the first simply uses different,

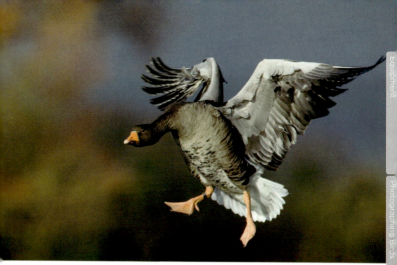

Cropping page 18

more processor-intensive routines to store data than the standard file formats (see LZW), the latter actually discards some data from the image. The best known lossy compression system is JPEG, which allows the user to choose how much data is lost as the file is saved.

CONTRAST
The range of tones across an image, from bright highlights to dark shadows.

CROPPING
The process of removing unwanted areas of an image, leaving behind the most significant elements.

DEPTH OF FIELD
The distance in front of and behind the point of focus in a photograph, in which the scene remains in acceptable sharp focus.

DIALOG BOX
An onscreen window, part of a program, for entering settings.

DIFFUSION
The scattering of light by a material, resulting in a softening of the light and of any shadows cast. Diffusion occurs in nature through mist and cloud cover, and can also be simulated using diffusion sheets and soft-boxes.

DIGITAL ZOOM
Many cheaper cameras offer a digital zoom function. This crops from the center of the image and scales the image up using image processing algorithms. Unlike a zoom lens, or "optical zoom," the effective resolution is reduced as the zoom level increases; 2× digital zoom uses ¼ of the image sensor area, 3× uses 1/9, and so on. The result is very poor image quality; even if you start with an eight megapixel sensor, at 3× digital zoom your image would be taken from less than one megapixel of it.

DPI (DOTS PER INCH)
A measurement of how many dots of ink a color printer can put down.

DYE SUBLIMATION PRINTER
A color printer that works by transferring dye images to a substrate (paper, card, etc.) by heat, to give near photographic-quality prints.

DYNAMIC RANGE
A measure of image density from the maximum recorded density to the minimum, so an image with a DMax (maximum density) of 3.1 and a DMin (minimum) of 0.2 would have a dynamic range of 2.9. Dynamic range is measured on a logarithmic scale: an intensity of 100:1 is 2.0, 1,000:1 is 3.0. The very best drum scanners can achieve around 4.0.

EDGE LIGHTING
Light that hits the subject from behind and slightly to one side, creating flare or a bright "rim lighting" effect around the edges of the subject.

EXTRACTION
In image editing, the process of creating a cut-out selection from one image for placement in another.

181

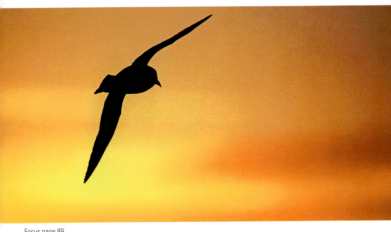

Focus page 89

FEATHERING

In image-editing, the fading of the edge of an image or selection.

FILE FORMAT

The method of writing and storing information (such as an image) in digital form. Formats commonly used for photographs include TIFF and JPEG.

FILL-IN FLASH

A technique that uses the on-camera flash or an external flash in combination with natural or ambient light to reveal detail in the scene and reduce shadows.

FILL LIGHT

An additional light used to supplement the main light source. Fill can be provided by a separate unit, or alternatively, a reflector.

FILTER

(1) A thin sheet of transparent material placed over a camera lens or light source to modify the quality or color of the light passing through. (2) A feature in an image-editing application that alters or transforms selected pixels for some kind of visual effect.

FOCAL LENGTH

The distance between the optical center of a lens and its point of focus when the lens is focused on infinity.

FOCAL RANGE

The range over which a camera or lens is able to focus on a subject (e.g., 0.5m to Infinity).

FOCUS

The optical state where the light rays converge on the film or sensor to produce the sharpest possible image.

FRINGE

In image-editing, an unwanted border effect to a selection, where the pixels combine some of the colors from inside the selection with some from the background.

F-STOP

The calibration of the aperture size of a photographic lens.

GAMMA

A measure of the contrast of an image, expressed as the steepness of the characteristic curve of an image.

GAMUT

The range of colors a device such as a monitor or printer can produce. Colors a device cannot produce are described as "out of gamut."

GIGABYTE

A unit of computer memory or data. One gigabyte (Gb) equals approximately 1,000 megabytes (Mb).

GRADUATION

The smooth blending of one tone or color into another, or from transparent to colored in a tint. A graduated lens filter, for instance, might be dark on one side, fading to clear at the other.

GRAYSCALE

An image made up of a sequential series of 256 gray tones, covering the entire gamut between black and white.

HALO

A bright line tracing the edge of an image. This is usually an anomaly of excessive digital processing to sharpen or compress an image.

HISTOGRAM

A map of the distribution of tones in an image, arranged as a graph. The horizontal axis goes from the darkest tones present to the lightest, while the vertical axis shows the number of pixels in that range.

HOT-SHOE

An accessory fitting found on most digital and film SLR cameras and some high-end compact models, normally used to control an external flash unit. Depending on the model of camera, passes information to lighting attachments via the metal contacts of the shoe.

HSB

(Hue, Saturation, Brightness) The three dimensions of color, and the standard color model used to adjust color in many image-editing applications.

HUE

The pure color defined by position on the color spectrum; what is generally meant by "color" in lay terms.

INCANDESCENT LIGHTING

This strictly means light created by burning, referring to traditional filament bulbs. They are also known as hotlights, since they remain on and become very hot.

ISO

An international standard rating for film speed, with the film getting faster as the rating increases. ISO 400 film is twice as fast as ISO 200, and will produce a correct exposure with less light and/or a shorter exposure. However, higher-speed film tends to produce more grain in the exposure.

JPEG

(Joint Photographic Experts Group) Pronounced "jay-peg," a system for compressing images, developed as an industry standard by the International Standards Organization. Compression ratios are typically between 10:1 and 20:1, although lossy (but not necessarily noticeable to the eye).

KELVIN

Scientific measure of temperature based on absolute zero (simply take 273.15 from any temperature in Celsius to convert to Kelvin). In photography measurements in Kelvin refer to color temperature. Unlike other measures of temperature, the degrees symbol in not used.

LASSO

In image-editing, a tool used to draw an outline around an area of an image for the purposes of selection.

LAYER

In image-editing, one level of an image file that is separate from the rest, allowing different elements to be edited separately.

LCD

(Liquid Crystal Display) Flat-screen display used in digital cameras and some monitors. A liquid-crystal solution held between two clear polarizing sheets is subject to an electrical current, which alters the alignment of the crystals so that they either pass or block the light.

LUMINOSITY

The brightness of a color, independent of the hue or saturation.

LZW

(Lempel-Ziv-Welch) A standard option when saving TIFF files which reduces file sizes, especially in images with large areas of similar color. This option does not lose any data from the image, but cannot be opened by some image editing programs.

MACRO

A mode offered by some lenses and cameras that enables the lens or camera to focus in extreme close-up.

MASK

In image-editing, a grayscale template that hides part of an image. One of the most important tools in editing an image, it is used to limit changes to a particular area or protect part of an image from alteration.

MEGABYTE

A unit of computer memory or data storage capacity equivalent to 1,024 kilobytes or 1,048,576 bytes of data.

MEGAPIXEL

A rating of resolution for a digital camera, directly related to the number of pixels forming or output by the CMOS or CCD sensor. The higher the megapixel rating is, the higher the resolution of images created by the camera will be.

MIDTONE

The parts of an image that are approximately average in tone, falling midway between the highlights and shadows.

NOISE

Random pattern of small spots on a digital image that are generally unwanted, caused by nonimage-forming electrical signals.

PIXEL

(PICture ELement) The smallest units of a digital image, pixels are the square screen dots that make up a bitmapped picture. Each pixel carries a specific tone and color.

PLUG-IN

In image-editing, software produced by a third party and intended to supplement a program's features or performance.

PPI (PIXELS PER INCH)

A measure of resolution for a bitmapped image.

PROCESSOR

A silicon chip containing millions of micro-switches, designed for performing specific functions in a computer or digital camera.

RAW FILES

A digital image format, known sometimes as the "digital negative," which preserves higher levels of color depth than traditional 8 bits per channel images. The image can then be adjusted in software—potentially by three stops—without loss of quality. The file also stores camera data including meter readings, aperture settings, and more. In fact each camera model creates its own kind of Raw file, though leading models are supported by software like Adobe Photoshop.

RESAMPLING

Changing the resolution of an image file either by removing pixels (lowering resolution) or adding them by interpolation (increasing resolution).

RESOLUTION

The level of detail in a digital image, measured in pixels (e.g. 1,024 by 768 pixels), or dots-per-inch (in a half-tone image only, i.e. 1200 dpi).

RGB

(Red, Green, Blue) The primary colors of the additive model, used in monitors and image-editing programs.

SATURATION

The purity of a color, going from the lightest tint to the deepest, most saturated tone.

SELECTION

In image editing, a part of an on-screen image that is chosen and defined by a border in preparation for manipulation or movement.

SHUTTER

The device inside a conventional camera that controls the length of time during which the film is exposed to light. Many digital cameras don't have a shutter, but the term is still used as shorthand to describe the electronic mechanism that controls the length of exposure for the sensor.

SHUTTER SPEED

The time the shutter (or electronic switch) leaves the sensor or film open to light during an exposure.

Telephoto page 29

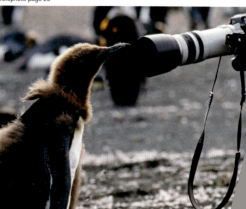

SLR

(Single Lens Reflex) A camera that transmits the same image via a mirror to the film and viewfinder, ensuring that you get exactly what you see in terms of focus and composition.

SPOT METER

A specialized light meter, or function of the camera light meter, that takes an exposure reading for a precise area of a scene.

TELEPHOTO

A photographic lens with a long focal length that enables distant objects to be enlarged. The drawbacks include a limited depth of field and limited angle of view.

TIFF

(Tagged Image File Format) A file format for bitmapped images. It supports CMYK, RGB and grayscale files with alpha channels, and lab, indexed-color, and it can use LZW lossless compression. It is now the most widely used standard for high resolution digital photographic images.

WHITE BALANCE

A digital camera control used to balance exposure and color settings for artificial lighting types.

ZOOM LENS

A camera lens with an adjustable focal length which gives, in effect, a range of lenses in one. Drawbacks compared to a prime lens include a smaller maximum aperture and increased distortion.

Shooting Low page 91

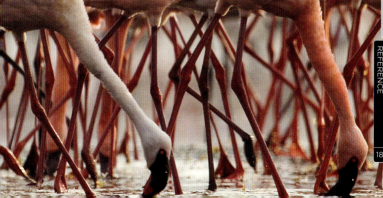

Index

action shots 49, 55, 63, 74, 98–9
adaptors 21, 22
Adobe 9, 121, 124, 126, 127, 128
see also Photoshop
air travel 112–13
albatrosses 32, 45, 72, 73
aluminum tripods 35
Antarctica 33, 72, 73, 103
aperture 23, 26, 28, 40, 41, 42, 43, 49, 52, 117
Aperture Priority 23
Apple 123, 124, 127, 128, 133
Arca Swiss 36
auklets 72, 73
autoexposure 111
autofocus (AF) 8, 23, 26, 30, 49, 88–9, 117
avocets 9

backdrops 65
background 23, 41, 52, 53, 65, 68, 84, 88, 90, 174
backlighting 94, 96
backyard birds 64–9, 84
baited sites 78–9
baiting 76, 81
bald eagles 53, 79
ball heads 36
ball-and-socket heads 36
barn owls 32, 33, 121, 144, 165
beanbags 38–9, 51, 90, 107, 111
bellows 47
binoculars 22
birds of prey 76–9
birdscapes 28
birdwatchers 21, 29, 170
bitterns 91

black grouse 80
black guillemots 146, 147, 148
black woodpeckers 108, 109
blackcaps 47
blimp 111
blinds 9, 28, 38, 64, 66, 73, 74, 76, 77, 78, 80, 82, 95, 104–9, 177
blinker function 46
bluebirds 66
blur 23, 48, 117
blurring motion 50–1, 89
boats 73
botanical gardens 71
breeding season 73, 81
Bridge 130, 131
brightness 44, 136
buffer 49
buntings 39, 102
burst depth 14, 19

calibration devices 128, 129
Camera Raw 141
camera shake 30, 51, 117
Canada geese 33, 71
Canon 13, 31, 61, 128
Canon 7D 14
Canon zoom 29
canvas blinds 64, 66
capercaillies 80, 81
captive birds 86–7
car ferries 73
carbon-fiber tripods 34
card readers 130, 131
center-weighted metering 23, 43
cities 70–1
cleaning 60–1
clipping 44, 45, 46, 47
Clone Stamp 86, 154–5
close-ups 20, 28
colonies 72–3, 74, 89

color profiles 128
colorimeter 128
color 126–9, 146–51
common crane 30, 31
common sandpipers 82
common terns 88
compact cameras 15–17, 21–2, 54
CompactFlash (CF) 54, 130
competitions 171
composition, improving 142–5
compressions 56, 117
computers 10, 19, 54, 120, 121, 122–4
Continuous AF 23
Continuous drive mode 23
contrast 137, 146–51, 160
converters 24, 25, 26, 30–1
crakes 80–1
cranes 28, 30, 31, 94, 95, 96, 97, 115
cropped sensors 18, 19
cropped-frame DSLR 32
cropping 25, 26, 31, 142–5
curlews 105, 116, 117
Curves 137–8, 149, 150, 151, 152–3

Dalmatian pelicans 142, 143, 154, 155
Dartford warblers 107
demoiselle cranes 115
depth of field 14, 28, 40, 41, 42, 48, 49, 52–3, 77, 84, 86, 99, 111
Detail 138
Dietmar Nil 37
digibinning 22
digiscoping 17, 20–3, 54, 116–17, 166
digital compact cameras 15
digital editing 59, 120–77

color profiles 128
digital single lens reflex (DSLR) 14, 15, 18–19, 32, 42, 43, 44, 49, 52, 116
digital zoom 22
dippers 48, 49, 118–19
display 80
divers 74
drinking pools 84, 85
drive mode 23
ducks 24, 40, 86, 118, 119
dummy lens 106
dust 60–1

eagles 53, 60, 76, 77, 78, 79, 86, 96
egrets 74, 114, 115
eider ducks 40, 118, 119
electronic viewfinder (EVF) 15
emperor penguins 44, 45, 90, 91, 103, 112, 113, 118
ethics 174–7
exposure 40–7, 58, 136, 146–51
exposure mode 23
exposure ratio 43
eye-level images 90
eyes 51, 53, 92, 159

f-stops 26, 28, 29, 30, 37, 41, 43, 52, 60
falconers 86
feeders 64, 65–7, 84, 110
field craft 63, 100–3
fieldfare 64, 65
fights 98, 99
file browsers 130, 131
file formats 56–9
file size 19
fill-in flash 92
fish eagles 78, 79
fish-eye lenses 32, 33

flamingos 50, 91
flight 8, 9, 28, 29, 31, 34, 37,
    42, 43, 48–9, 50, 80,
    88–9, 118–19
floating blinds 74
fluid heads 36
focal length 14, 17, 21, 26,
    30, 49
focus 23, 41, 52, 117
focus mode 23
focusing 14, 26, 89, 117
focusing distance 26
frames per second 19, 49
freezing action 15, 26, 42,
    48–9, 79, 99
full-frame sensors 18, 19

game birds 80–1
gardens 64–9
geese 18, 19, 28, 33, 71, 74,
    75
gimbal-style heads 37
Giotto bulb blower 60–1
Gitzo 34, 35
goldcrests 26, 31
golden eagles 60, 76, 77, 86
golden plovers 83
goldfinches 66
goshawks 95
grain 42, 46
gray herons 98, 99
great bustards 40, 92, 93,
    174
great spotted woodpeckers
    65, 66, 110
great tinamou 149
grebes 74, 75
green sandpipers 82
greenshank 82
grouse 39
gulls 20, 21, 73

handheld shots 31, 34, 72,

89
hard drives 124
hawfinches 85
hawk owls 42, 48
Healing Brush 140, 154–5
heat haze 117
herons 24, 52, 53, 74, 98,
    99, 124, 125
high-impact images 53
highlights 46, 47, 153
histograms 44–7, 146
hoopoes 102, 103
horizon 91
horned grebe 74, 75
HSL/Grayscale 139
hummingbirds 26, 59, 66,
    68, 93

ICC profiles 128
image quality 23
Image Rescue 130
image-stabilized lenses 51
importing 130–3
Internet 55, 61
interpolating 156
iPhoto 133
ISO 23, 30, 40, 42, 43, 79,
    116

JPEG files 54, 56, 58–9, 116
JPEG Fine 23, 58

kestrels 48, 77
Kew Gardens 71
king eider 118, 119
king penguins 12, 29, 115
kinglets 26
Kirk Enterprises 38
kites 78, 150, 151
kittiwakes 70–1
knots 41, 63, 82, 83

lakes 70

landscapes 28
laptops 124
lawns 70
LCD screen 15–16, 44, 46,
    47, 110
leks/lekking 80, 83
lens corrections 140
lens covers 61
lens hood 94
lens shake 21, 51
lenses 13, 17, 18, 22, 24–9,
    30–1, 32–3, 49, 51, 52,
    61, 73, 89, 94
Levels 147
Lexar 130
licenses 76, 104, 176, 177
lighting 92–7
Lightroom 127, 128, 141
long telephoto 13, 24, 52,
    84
loons 42, 43
lossy format 56
low shots 90–1
Lumix DMC-G1 15–16

Macro 23
magnification 21
Manfrotto 34
manual focus 89
matrix metering 43
medium telephoto 13, 17,
    28, 29
medium zoom 28, 29
memory cards 19, 23, 54–5,
    58, 130
mergansers 87, 101
metering 23, 41, 43, 111,
    117
Micro Four Thirds cameras
    15–17
migration 79, 82, 85, 88
mobbing 102
monitor shades 117

monopods 35
mood 50, 52
motion blur 50–1, 71
mudflats 82
multipattern metering 43
mute swans 75, 98

nest photography 104, 105
NEX cameras 16, 17
Nikkor AF-S lens 26
Nikon 13, 26, 30, 31, 61,
    128
Nikon Coolpix 22, 117
noise 30, 42–3, 45, 46

observation decks 28
Olympus 16
opening up 41
optical zoom 22
orioles 66
ospreys 51, 76, 79, 120, 176
out-of-focus foreground 52,
    86, 90
output formats 156–7
overexposure 44, 46
owls 9, 32, 33, 42, 48, 78,
    87, 111, 121, 144, 165,
    170

paddyfield warblers 85
pan-and-tilt heads 36
Panasonic 15–16
panning 51
parasitic jaeger 28, 29, 60,
    61
parks 32, 33, 70, 71, 90
partridges 81
passerines 84–5
PC card adapter 130
pelicans 142, 143, 154, 155
penguins 6, 7, 12, 13, 29,
    33, 44, 45, 90, 91, 103,
    112, 113, 115, 118

petrels 73, 89

phalaropes 59, 100, 101

pheasants 71, 81

Photoshop 46, 92, 96, 117, 130, 141

Photoshop Elements 9, 121, 124, 126, 133

Picasa 133

pigeons 70, 71

pixel count 19

pixels 15, 19, 22, 44, 46, 47, 56, 146, 156

plovers 83

plug-ins 58

plumage 40, 44, 46, 58, 93

ponds 67

poor light 42

printing 162–5

processing 19, 56, 58, 92, 116

processing a Raw image 134–41

processing speeds 17, 49

ptarmigan 102, 103

publication 166–71

puffins 11, 72, 89, 157, 158, 175

purple gallinule 80, 81

quick-release plates 37, 88

rails 80–1

RAM 122

raptors 76–9, 86

Raw 23, 54, 56, 58–9, 96, 122, 127

recovery options 55

redwings 173

remote release lead 21

remote-control photography 110–11

renumbering 133

reserves 38, 64, 82, 104

resizing 156–7

rim lighting 96

roadrunners 16, 17, 34, 35

robins 19, 66, 67, 84, 85, 152, 153

rookeries 74

roseate spoonbills 129

Ross's geese 28

ruffs 83

running 50

St. James's Park 32, 33, 70, 71

Samsung 16–17

sand 60

sanderlings 102

sandhill cranes 28, 97

sandpipers 26, 27, 82

saturation 137

scanners 123

sea eagles 78, 79

seabirds 72–3

secondhand cameras 13

Secure Digital (SD) 54

self-timer 117

sensors 14, 15, 16, 17, 18, 19, 30, 42, 43, 48, 60, 61

shadows 46, 94, 136, 153

sharpening 158–61

shorebirds 82–3, 102, 105

short telephoto 13

shrikes 25

shrubs 69, 70

shutter lag 22

shutter speed 21, 23, 30, 40, 41, 42, 43, 48, 49, 50, 52, 79, 89, 99, 117

shutter-release cable 117

Siberian jay 96, 97

Sidekick 37

sidelighting 94

signal noise 42–3, 45

silhouettes 63, 94, 95, 96–7

Single AF 23

Single Shot mode 23

skuas 98

slide show 130, 131

snipe 82

snow 45, 46, 48, 53, 60, 96, 97, 103

snow geese 28, 75

software 58, 126–8, 130, 132

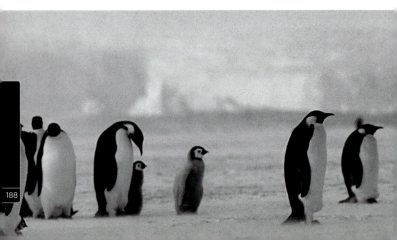

Sony 16–17, 124, 129
sorting 130–3
sparrows 66, 67
spectrophotometer 128
specular highlights 44
spoonbills 74, 129
spot metering 23, 41, 43, 117
stalking 63, 74, 82, 84, 100–3, 108
stone curlews 105
stopping down 41, 60
stops 40
storage 54, 172–3
storks 74, 98, 99
striated caracaras 113
superwide lenses 32
swab kit 61
swans 46, 74, 75, 98

tame birds 28, 32, 72
tanagers 66, 68
tape playback 81, 85, 102
tawny owls 87, 111

teleconverters 24, 25, 26, 30–1
telephoto 13, 17, 22, 24–7, 28, 34, 37, 52
telescopes 21, 22
Temminck's tragopan 86, 87
Tennessee warbler 58
terns 55, 73, 88, 119, 145
thrushes 64, 65, 66, 173
TIFFs 56, 58
tits 64, 66
Tone Curve 137
towns 70–1
trees 69
triggers 110–11
tripod heads 36–7, 38
tripods 21, 30, 34–5, 51, 90, 100, 101, 108, 111, 117

underexposure 44, 46, 47
urban environments 70–1
USB ports 54, 130

vacations 114–15

vehicles 38, 39, 107–8
video heads 36
viewfinder 21, 22, 36, 41, 49, 90
vignetting 21, 22, 140

waders 9, 24, 48, 82
warblers 16, 24, 58, 84, 85, 102, 107
water 67, 84, 85
water rails 81
waterbirds 70, 74–5, 97
weather 13, 34, 60
wetlands 74
white 44, 45, 46, 89
white balance 23, 56, 58, 135
white-crowned sparrow 66, 67
white-throated dippers 48, 49, 118, 119
whooper swans 46, 74
wide-angle lenses 32–3
wildfowl 74–5, 86, 90, 105

willow warbler 16
Wilson's phalaropes 100, 101
Wimberley 37, 51
window mounts 38–9
wing tips 48, 99
wiping cards 55
wireless transmitter 110
wood sandpipers 26, 27
woodland 70
woodlarks 84, 85
woodpeckers 65, 66, 108, 109, 110
workflow-based software 127
write speed 55

zoom 13, 22, 28–9, 30–1
zoos 86

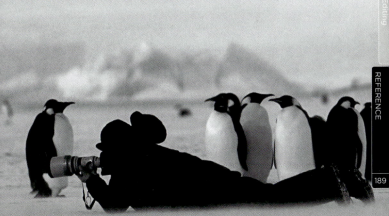

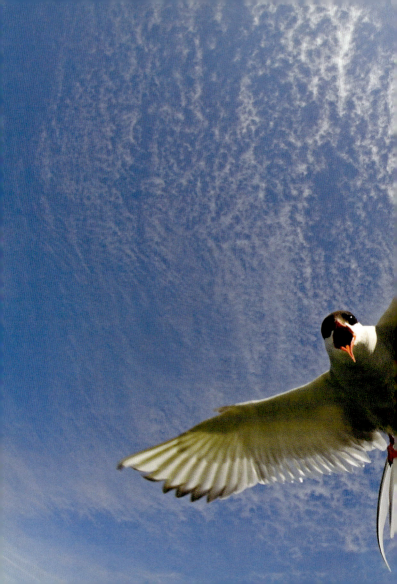

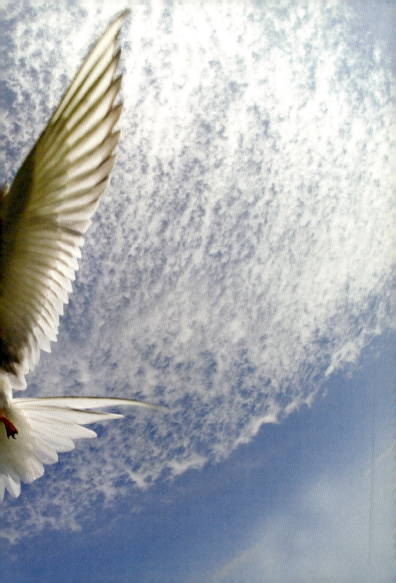

Picture Credits

Birds of Prey page 77

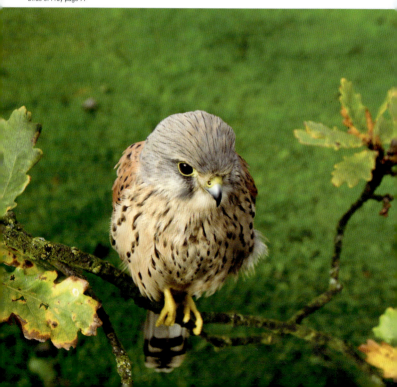